infoChina
The complete

SHANGHAI

P.T. Smallbone.

Tourist Publications

Published in the United Kingdom by
T P Books & Print Ltd
11a East Street
Leighton Buzzard
Bedfordshire LU7 8HU
United Kingdom
In association with
Tourist Publications
6 Piliou Street
Koliatsou Square
112 55 Athens

Copyright © Tourist Publications 1989

Produced by
T P Books & Print Ltd
in Australia

Editorial Directors: L. Starr, Y. Skordilis
Typography: Deblaere Typeseting Pty Ltd
Layout: Bookcraft Pty Ltd
Photo-setting: Deblaere Typesetting Pty Ltd
Authors: K. & G. Kenihan
                       N. Bliss
Photographs: William Torrens Pty Ltd
Colour Separations: Chroma Graphics
Maps: Lovell Johns Ltd

Printed in Singapore

ISBN 960 7587 14 6

Due to the wealth of information available it has been necessary
to be selective. Sufficient detail is given to allow the visitor to
make choices depending on personal taste, and the information
has been carefully checked. However, errors creep in an
changes will occur. We hope you will forgive the errors and
omissions and find this book a helpful companion.

ABOUT THIS GUIDE

Shanghai, the Paris of the East, fifth largest city on earth, China's leading commercial centre, there are many descriptions of Shanghai. But there is probably only one mood, romantic polite, relax, easy going in this fascinating and exotic city. This guide offers you all what you need.

Part I gives general information about China and Shanghai, including history, culture, government, geology, climate, flora, fauna etc.

Part II offers conveniently described sightseeing both in and out of Shanghai, arranged, for both a casual tour or a more detailed inspection; you pick what you want.

Part III consists of a full accommodation listing with useful additional information.

Part IV is full of practical information, starting before you arrived and taking you through shopping and eating, getting around and a page or two for 'Help!'

Part V is a special section for Business visitors. Colour maps of the area have been included.

We hope you have a wonderful time in Shanghai and that you will love it as we do, honouring her virtues and forgiving her faults. She is unique and special.

Acknowledgements

We would like to thank Mr Mark King, specialist in individual and special interest groups throughout China and Asia from Travel Asia Limited, 30-32 D'Aguilar Street, Hong Kong and Mr Peter Vanderhoorst of Travman Tours, 8 Whitehorse Road, Ringwood, Victoria, Australia for their provision of valuable information.

Table of Contents

PART I
General Introduction

CHINA AND HER PEOPLE

A CRADLE OF CIVILISATION

To the people of the western world, the vast land of eastern Asia which we know as China, has been and, in many ways still is, a source of mystery and fascination.

Part of this mystique is a misconception that Chinese civilisation is the oldest on earth. This is untrue. Certainly, cradles of neolithic civilisation had emerged in the river valleys of China between 10,000 and 6,000 BC. But there are parallels of the transition from nomadic hunters to emerging agriculture and stock husbandry in other great river valleys of the world – the Indus, the Euphrates and the Nile.

Before the discovery of metals, the pottery, bone and stone artifacts of all of these late Stone Age people, while differing in style, fulfilled identical social and community roles.

Present day tourists to China are able to see one of the world's best preserved neolithic sites just a few kilometres from the centre of the important western city of Xian. The excavated village of the ancient Banpo people is a time capsule which illustrates the slow transition towards a communal politic which, across at least three millenia, tranformed into the first flowering of what, today, is truly defined as civilisation.

Because of its isolation from the classical civilisations of Europe, the Middle East and Egypt, China has always been accredited with a history somewhat out of proportion with reality. It is only in this century that experiences of China have been within the reach of the western visitor rather than Christian missioneries and intrepid traders who were among the first Caucasians to venture into its cities and vast hinterland.

The first identifiable State structure is identified with the Shang Dynasty which dates from 1,600 BC. and is contemporaneous with the very advanced western civilisations exemplified by the cultures which flourished along the Nile, on the Mediterranean island of Crete and Asia Minor.

But from the commencement of the Shang period, China experienced more than one thousand years of small and constantly warring petty kingdoms until its first meaningful unification by the Emperor Qin from whose European-corrupted name **Chin,** this great land takes its name – China.

In his brief reign from 221 BC to 206 BC, when classical Greece was in its glorious Golden Age, the Emperor's subjects, as ignorant of the west as the west was of them, called their land the Middle Kingdom. They were firm in the belief that they occupied the centre of the world.

Two centuries later, imperial Rome had vague and rumored knowledge of a great empire far beyond the rising sun. Some of China's products, in particular silk cloth, reached the courts of the Caesars and, through Rome, found their way to the furthest outposts of the Roman empire.

The unique fabric resulted in the first recorded European name for the Chinese – Seres – **the People of Silk.**

Following the fall of Rome, the trade with China was continued by

9

the eastern empire of Byzantium through the tenuous links of Arab and Indian traders but one thousand years and 10 great Chinese dynasties were to pass before the Polo brothers of Venice and then Marco Polo brought to a western Europe emerging from its dark ages the first true accounts of Chinese civilisation and culture.

Unfortunately, Marco Polo's stories were so fantasised by the writing of his biographer Rustichello that, 350 years after the great adventurer's death, a Jesuit priest Matteo Ricci was still seeking the location of Marco Polo's wonderful land of Cathay. He was ignorant of having lived in it for several years.

The Jesuit's confusion is historically understandable in the light of the European Renaissance with its accompanying giant strides in so many areas of thought and art. The Renaissance had effectively narrowed the gap between Marco Polo's highly embellished world of Kublai Khan and the 16th century courts of China's Ming emperors.

The misconceptions of China continued for another two centuries – not with the traders and adventurers who saw for themselves – but in the philosophical debate of European intellectuals. They continued to attribute to China's rulers and bureaucrats a sophistication and glory which, in reality, could no longer compare with that of 18th century Europe.

Whatever remaining awe in which Europeans held the Chinese was soon to be blown away from the muzzle of the gun as the colonising nations of the west rapidly discovered that the military power of the Qing emperors ruling from 1644 was no match for the products of the industrial revolution.

One thousand years of admiration took less than 50 years to turn into effective contempt as the Great Powers – France, England, Russia, Germany, Portugal and, even the United States of America – successfully imposed humiliating concession trade treaties on a vast and immensely rich nation which did not possess the power to militarily oppose them.

Shanghai's foreign enclaves, with their varied European architectural styles, is typical of this era – the last decades of the 19th century through to 1949.

The effective end of the Chinese imperial history came in 1900 with the Boxer Rebellion although the Qing Dynasty was to live for 11 more pitiful,puppet years as a ghost echo of its former glory under the last emperor of China.

In 1911, a group of intellectuals in the Yangtze river city of Wuhan, looking to western cultural and industry as their country's only salvation, struck a small spark of revolution which engulfed imperial China like a forest fire.

In the 48 years between this republican revolution to the establishment of the People's Republic of China in 1949, the country continued to be politically cowered and practical dismembered by the enroachments and invasions of Russian and Japanese armies.

From 1949 until 1976, China closed its windowless doors to the world and, in some ways, the development of China in this 27-year period, was as much a mystery to the west as the court of the Mongol Emperor had been to the kings of Marco Polo's Europe.

Only in the past 14 years has the western world been gaining and ever-increasing insight into the manner in which more than 1.2 billion people have progressively built a unique society and future in the second half of the 20th century.

Geology and Geography

China is bordered by the USSR, North Korea, India, Nepal, Bhutan, Burma, Laos and Vietnam.

Next to the Soviet Union and Canada, China is, by area, the third largest nation on earth. Like the USSR, this vast country has dramatic changes in climate and scenery.

Because of this, the easiest way to divide China for the visitor is not by its provinces or even its major cities but to look at it in terms of geographic and climatic areas.

In this context, there are four Chinas — the north east, north west, south east and south west. To these must be added the Tibetan Autonomous Region, the fabled ' Roof of the World.'

China's geography is dominated by three great river systems, each of which rise in the mountain ranges in the west and run roughly eastward to the China Sea on which Shanghai is situated.

The northern area of China is drained by the Hwang-ho or Yellow River. The central half of the nation is influenced by the Changjiang or Yangtze River which rises below Mount Geladangdong on the Quinghai-Tibet plataau and rushes for more than 6.300 kilometres until it reaches its destiny by bustling Shanghai.

Southern China is drained by the Si Kiang or West River.

The mighty Yangtze is the most important to China's economy and, with its tributaries and maze of canals in its delta area, provides

Wuxia Gorge in Yangtze river

navigable water for a total of more than 32,000 kilometres. The basin of the Yangtze river is China's richest and most productive area.

The concentration of agriculture coupled with the relatively easy transportation that China's great rivers provide has resulted in the emergence of great cities such as Shanghai and Canton (Guangzhou.)

China can be divided as well between the very mountainous southern areas and the flatter north but there are also similar distinctions between the east and the west. In the north, the coastal plain is approximately only 650 kilometres at its widest before the emergence of rugged uplands.

The wind-blown alluvial soil is very deep and rich but agricultural production is limited by rainfall and water available for irrigation.

Visitors are entranced by the high shark-toothed mist-shrouded mountains along the Yangtze and rivers in the south east. The scenery is reflected in subtle, gentle paintings which are traditional art works in China. It comes as a surprise to some tourists that these works are not stylised at all.

The geology of China is dominated by two mountainous areas – one extending in a general east west line into central Asia, the other following a north east-south west pattern in the coastal regions. Both structural axes intersect with one another and, because of this structural complexity. rocks of all geological ages are widely, though irregularly, distributed.

The only significant areas of relatively undisturbed strata are found in the intervening basins where the thickness of the sedimentary rocks is great.

Climate and Temperature

A visitor might swear he's never felt colder, more wind-whipped than on the Great Wall out of Beijing in December and January. The oppressiveness of heat and humidity can also be claimed for the central and southern coastal areas in July.

The very size of China dictates vast climatic variations made even more complex by local conditions governed by variations in altitude.

Its hard to generalise but, the northern hemisphere's spring and autumn periods will present most of China at its most pleasant best.

Spring gardens and blossoming trees and russet, yellow and gold leaves being shed in autumn are spectacular in these beautiful seasons.

Winters in the north are harsh but there is something to be said for seeing it blanketed with snow. In the capital, Beijing, summer temperatures can soar beyond 38C (100F.) The main rainfall is in July and August.

In Shanghai and the Yangtze valley, semi-tropical conditions prevail. The summer is long and hot and can be extremely unpleasant in the river cities of Nanjing, Wuhan and Chonquing. The Chinese nickname for these cities is 'the three furnaces.'

Humidity is high in Shanghai throughout the year and the average rainfall is just over 1,100 millimetres (45 inches.)

Flora and Fauna

The natural flora of China is a spectrum of vegetation ranging from the sparse and stunted grasses and bushes of tundra and desert in the north and north west to rain forests in the south and south west.

There are still great areas of natural hard-wood forests in the north-eastern areas of China with deciduous oak the major growth. They mix with ash, elm and walnut. Evergreen oak forest extend over the mountain and hill areas of the south and south west while dense rain forest occurs along the southern frontiers.

Coniferous forests are encountered also in the north east, particularly in the regions bordered by North Korea and pines of many types are abundant in the south western plateau areas of China.

The great grassland areas stretch from the north east westward to the Tien Shan mountains.

China is also famed for its wildflowers that have become cultivated and prized in the western world – the wild roses and lilacs in the north are outstanding examples.

The diversity of fauna in China is greatest throughout the mountainous regions of the west which is the natural habitat of the **Giant Panda** now one of the world's most endangered species.

In the north east, there are relations with the animal life of the Siberian forests while the deserts of the Mongolian Autonomous Region are inhabited by animals from central Asia.

The south east and south west have a diversity of species of reptiles, amphibians, birds and mammals that are typical of the tropical regions of south east Asia.

The Chinese people have always been fascinated by the fauna of other lands and take pride in their zoos. The great collections of animals in the zoos of the large cities such as Beijing, Shanghai and Guangzhou are inevitable attractions for the foreign visitor and a constant source interest and recreation to the Chinese themselves.

While you'll see dogs in the rural areas, they, with cats, are relatively rare sights in Shanghai and the other great cities – unless you visit one of the increasing numbers of free markets. There, they are caged and waiting for the chef.

The concept of the domestic pet is basically foreign to China with the exception of caged birds and goldfish.

China's great rivers are sources of wide dispersal of the carp family and the cat fish, both of which are good eating. Natural bird life is prolific in most areas, both indigenous and migratory.

Government

What makes the central government of China tick? It is still surrounded by an aura of mystery beyond the reality that ultimate power is the prerogative of the Standing Committee of the Communist Party Politbureau's 25 members who, in turn, direct the Central Committee's membership of more than 200.

These representatives are, in general, party luminaries from the nation's provinces and outstandingly talented younger party members.

The power of the Party pervades every area of government and is recognisable in education, industry, transport and the armed forces in particular. The practical administration of China is the responsibility of the State Council which is, of, course, directly responsible to the Communist Party. The Council's titular head is the Premier who has four vice-Premiers and 10 State Councillors assisting him.

The Council's secretary general is charged with practically implementing the directions of the party's Politbureau in all areas of China's agriculture, industry, internal commerce and external trade through 45 ministeries.

Then, there's the National People's Congress which, in theory, chooses the Premier of the State Council and can even change the constitution. In practice, there's a Catch 22 situation because anything the NPC may decide must first be recommended by the Central Committee.

The virtually pre-determined decisions of the National People's Congress, whose large membership embraces a spectrum of technocrats, intellectuals and industrial management – the military being almost conspicuous by its absence – may seem unimportant to the western observer. Not so to the Chinese where the paper tiger, ie the NPC, maintains an illusion of grass roots democracy that is constantly disseminated through China's internal and external media.

The practical administration of China's largest cities is typified by the local government of Shanghai. It, like Beijing and Tianjin, is a municipality under the direct jurisdiction of the central government. Currently, Shanghai with its 10 urban counties covers 6,185 square kilometres with a population exceeding 12 million, more than half of which is concentrated in an area of roughly 230 square kilometres.

This extremely high density is responsible for Shanghai's chronic and seemingly insoluble housing problem and results in the bustling crowds of the down town area.

Lunch time

Education

Among the greatest achievements of the People's Republic of China has been the almost passionate pursuit of public education of its currently estimated 1.5 billion people and the eradication of illiteracy.

In theory, elementary education is available to the children of the smallest and most isolated villages and the most informed estimate between central government claims and western observation now places more than half of China's population in the literacy sphere.

The Central Committee is constantly aware that less than five million of the people who have university degrees and the current 1.7 million receiving **tertiary education** is an insignificant contribution to the scientific and technical needs of the nation.

Probably because of Shanghai's importance in China's industry, transport, internal commerce and foreign trade, the city has fared better than most educationally. The municipal administration presently claims a total enrolment of all school aged children with education compulsory to the third grade of what can be loosely termed junior high school.

The city boasts nearly 200 tertiary colleges, universities and institutions of technical and scientific research. The two outstanding institutions are the universities of **Jiaotong** and **Fudan**.

More than 30,000 of Shanghai's population are directly involved in education and the city's medical training and health research programs are the largest and most important in the nation.

Economically centred as it is on relatively light manufacturing industries, Shanghai exerts constant pressure for trade and technical teaching. The city has been in the forefront of night and part-time education enabling unskilled workers to acquire progressively technical know-how unavailable to them in their work places.

The city also boasts an enlightened **Science and Technical Exchange** institution where industrial workers regularly meet to evaluate and swap trade and scientific information developed in their places of work.

Commerce and Industry

In the first years of the 19th century, the armies of Napoleon Bonaparte had briefly conquered Egypt and the eyes of the Emperor, like those of Alexander long before him, turned eastward to further conquests.

Beyond India to Cathay.

It was then that Napoleon's Grand Marshall Ney uttered his historic prophesy:

'China is a sleeping giant, Sire. Let the giant sleep for, when it wakes, the world will tremble.'

The nations of the west are not trembling yet
but the dramatic reforms in every area of Chinese
economy – industry, agriculture, science and
technology – are progressively geared to turn the People's Republic into a modern State by the dawn of the 21st century.

The practical achievement of this goal stems from the early 1960s when a policy of 'Four Modernisations' was laid down, aimed at just about everything four-fold by the year 2000.

The PRC turned in upon itself at the end of the civil war in 1949 and, under Mao Tse Dong, China isolated itself from global economy. Everything was sub-serviant to the revolutionary leader's fears that economic contact with the world beyond China would result in dependency on international economics and increasing pressure for a return to capitalism.

Later, the **Cultural Revolution** sounded the death knell of the most elementary aspects of private enterprise in China and every facet of the nation from the lowliest village eating house to the emerging nuclear industry came firmly under centralised State control.

The result of the Cultural Revolution was, in hindsight, little short of catastrophic.

The failure of Mao's isolationist economy has progressively resulted in the current three-level system, each level of which is still essentially controlled by the central government.

The control of consumer staples such as cereals, edible oils and the major industrial raw materials is still the responsibility of the State. But below this level is a secondary area of private buying of goods and services where a price-range is recommended, if not controlled, by the State.

Below this again is an increasingly emerging area of free trade in which the prices are determined between the opposing needs of the buyer and the seller. But the free markets are still subject to State intervention as and when unfair or exploitive trade practices emerge.

The most fundamental differences that have occured in the 1980s have been the policies of returning an increasing number of managerial decisions back to factory managers who now are responsible for acquiring their own raw materials, their own workers and setting such things as overtime rates and production bonuses.

There have been far-reaching rural reforms as well. And, in the mid-1980s, a system was introduced by which farmers could acquire land on long-term leases with the rights to even transfer those lease-holds to others who could pay for them.

The emergence of the colourful free markets has also encouraged agricultural workers to increase their production although the State still maintains rigid control of grain and cotton production.

Currently China is increasingly looking to loans from western banks, other sources of foreign investment and, particularly in tourism, the benefits of joint ventures with western experts in this industry – mainly hotels.

In 1985, Shanghai and Guangzhou (Canton) were chosen for a dramatic shift from rigid centralised price controls and prices dictated by supply and demand in those cities appear to have been a successful experiment which will be progressively extended over the next decade.

In Shanghai, modern economic and cultural developments began earlier than in other regions. Machine building, the textile industry, printing and the cinema began in Shanghai which also produced China's first newspaper.

Although Shanghai is still a major force in China's economy, its growth rate has been overtaken by Beijing and Guangzhou. One of the city's problems has been the progressive pressure of essential infrastructures of water reticulation, sewerage disposal, road building – all those essential municipal services which were not significantly expanded after the British and French eras of the 1930s.

Yet, among more than 160 officially standardised categorised industries in China, Shanghai is actively engaged in 145.

The major areas include metallurgical, chemical and machine and electrical engineering industries, shipbuilding, electronics, textile and pharmaceutical manufacturing, with a huge diversity of light industry.

Religion

After the death of Mao Tse Dong, who professed atheism because all religions were superstitious plots which supposedly maintained strength among dominant, ruling classes, China began to relent on the firm banning of all religious practices.

Despite the revolutionary period in which temples and monasteries were destroyed or used for other purposes. Some ties, even reflective, were maintained by Buddhist and Muslim people with old philosophies.

And, with the still delicate situation in Tibet, these groups, along with Lamaists have been allowed to resume religious activities. However, these remain under State control.

Philosophies propounded by the founders of **Taoism, Confucianism** and **Buddhism** previously had encouraged followers rather than any specifial concept of religion, even though each founder was deified.

Beliefs were interwoven with worship of disciples and the spirits of ancestors which made for a rich and complicated tapestry.

There were gods, also, which represented divinities of various professions. Today, it is difficult to assess the impact of traditional religions in China, although certain ceremonies such as pasting paper effigies on doors in southern China and incense-burning pilgrimages have been revived.

The Chinese are more imbued with achieving material success than following through superstitious predictions of the future and being beholden to the actions of dead spirits.

Descendents of Chinese Jews formerly principally located in Hunan Province still consider themselves as Jews, although beliefs and customs associated with Judaism have become obsolete.

The Christian missionaries of the 19th century were regarded as being used by the Western world to increase its influence and also seemed a threat to traditional moral, scientific, educational and religious traditions of the Chinese people.

Christianity was not buried by the 1949 communist emergence but along with Buddhist temples, Christian churches had their doors forcibly closed during the Cultural Revolution.

Today, there are about 6 million Christians in China but the government will not acknowledge the Pope as the leader of the Catholic Church. This is exacerbated by the fact that diplomatic relations are maintained with the Vatican by Taiwan.

> **INFOTIP:** In Shangha , Catholic, Protestant and Moslem services can be attended at numerous churches and mosques. But no synagogues remain as the previously strong Jewish community no longer exists.

The Chinese People

The people of China can be hard to get to know. This is not because the approximate 93 per cent of **Han people** nor the 55 other minorities, including Mongols and Tibetans, are essentially unfriendly.

Language/languages remain a huge problem in a huge nation and, also, the westerner is still a strange enough body even in the big cities as to attract dumbfounded, staring responses from those not directly associated with the hospitality industry.

While there is evidence in Chinese myths, traditions, archaeology and earliest history that the Han people came to what is known is China via **Singkiang** or Chinese Turkistan, other scholars have conjectured that they entered China from the north. Certainly, the Chinese people originally ecpanded from what is now north central China, rapidly extending their influence over the rest of the country and contributing the Han traits to adjacent nations such as the Koreans, some Japanese and the Indo Chinese people.

The skin colour of the Chinese, while generally best described as light yellow, can be quite fair in some areas and brownish in others. But the hair is invariable jet black and straight and the Mongolian eye-fold is conspicuous.

The Han people are usually of medium height although, in some northern areas, it is not unusual to see adult males close to two metres tall.

The greatest concentration of aboriginal tribes in China is in the south west while, in the north and north west, other non-Chinese groups, principally the **Mongols** are in large numbers and have not greatly assimilated with the Han people.

Other minorities include the **Tungus people** believed to be closely related more to the aboriginal tribes of Siberia than to the Mongols while in Sinkiang Arabs, Turks, Uighurs and Kazaks have traditionally lived side by side with their Han neighbours.

The basis of Chinese society has always been the family system which, for four millenia dominated almost every aspects of Chinese society including its economic and political life.

This reverence of the family unit has not suffered greatly with the supremacy of Communist ideology in modern China. But it is now under serious threat as the central government seeks to contain the nation's previously exploding population through the one-child family policy backed by the nation-wide availability of birth control measures and legal abortion.

Again, because of language difficulties, visitors may not have much exchange with the ordinary people.

> **INFOTIP:** People who have not had much contact with westerners still consider it impolite to be touched in gestures of spontaneous affection in the making of new friendships or even during the telling of a joke. Try to contain natural gestures, particularly the patting on the head of a child.

Since the end of the fear which accompanied the end of the Cultural Revolution, more people in positions in the hospitality industry are willing to tell how things were and to try to extend their horizons vicariously into the west – which can make for very intersting exchanges.

But contact with the west has also produced some of the changing attitudes Mao Tse Dong predicted and feared.

It is natural that the apparent wealth of some western visitors should be noted. Tipping, which was once strictly forbitten, is now acceptable and even encouraged in cities like Shanghai. This is also a result of some Chinese hotel staff having trained in the west under joint venture schemes.

But tips should not be too lavish.

Han Man

Meeting People

A slight bow, perhaps nothing more than a downwards incline of the head coupled with the conventional handshake is now recognised by all Chinese as a polite greeting.

But the Chinese do not associate the strength of a handgrip with either sincerity of preferred friendship nor masculinity. It's not necessary to offer a Chinese a limp-fish handshake but the bone-crusher variety is not understood.

On first encounters, you'll get the hang of things by feeling the pressure of your Chinese host or friend's grip and take this as a guide from then on.

Embracing, as stated before, is out unless you have made a particular and deep friend who has become aware of the customs in your country.

Latin-style hand-kissing, man to woman, may not produce resentment but, instead, bewildered embarrassment and, perhaps, gales of laughter from onlookers.

In summer, do not offend the Chinese by wearing anything too skimpy. Shanghai is probably the most tolerant towards most forms of western fashion trends but people in regions less accustomed to visitors could have their sensibilities upset by too briefly cut garments.

Retaining or losing face is still a very important facet of Chinese life. Even in the major hotels and restaurants of China's largest cities, angry confrontation with a desk clerk, waiter or domestic staff can bring more than irritating frustration. Example: You may see people at an adjoining table eating a particular dish and be told by your waiter that it is not available.

Reacting angrily and, particularly, loudly is not the solution to this situation. It's not really relevant if you or he or she have made a mistake. What is important is that the Chinese waiter or waitress will lose face if a scene is created by the guest.

The louder the guest's protests, the less likely the service will be forthcoming. Quiet and polite persistence is a better way to go. In this example, it might well result in the attendant saving face by moving to another area of the establishment and the replacement providing the dishes requested.

Chinese Language

Travellers who have had few problems in learning basic phrases in European languages other than English are often deterred from attempting the most simple communications in Chinese.

Before the creation of the People's Republic of China, you would have been in even greater trouble because Chinese was not one language but several. While the two most generally used were **Mandarin** in the north and **Cantonese** in the south, there were six others in general use. They still are and a Chinese in southern China may not understand the speech of a native from the north. Both would have great difficulty understanding a citizen of Shanghai speaking that city's language.

Winter Dusk

The people of Shanghai are a distinctive group whose language reflects their pride in their lifestyle differing from other cities and regions.

It is difficult to describe their language but perhaps best distinction can be made by describing other languages of China as sounding monosyllabic while Shanghaiese is more polysyllabic on the ears.

For a long time, the people of Shanghai attempted to resist the central government's bid to encourage them to speak only Mandarin, which is a universally accepted dialect.

It is probably easiest for the visitor to learn a few phrases in Mandarin for it is widely understood by 70 per cent of all Chinese including those from Shanghai. The same phrases would be equally useful in other areas of China.

Mandarin is the official language of China. It is taught in all schools and is used on all national radio and television broadcasts. Written Chinese is the same everywhere.

If Mandarin was written phonetically, it would look quite different from Cantonese or Shanghaiese in much the same way that written English looks different from written German or French. This is because the Chinese written language does not use a phonetic script indicating sounds but characters indicating syllables or words.

This system can be traced back to simple ideographs that probably had their beginnings in the late neolithic period. The Chinese language needed to be transliterated into the Roman alphabet for westerners to even attempt to speak it.

The first significant attempt at this was produced by a Thomas Wade and his collaborator Herbert Giles and while it was more accurate than earlier systems, their approach was succeeded by a Chinese phonetic alphabet.

This is called the **pinyin system** which has been used in all texts since 1979. It is a fairly accurate attempt to provide a neutral set of symbols to represent definite sounds and it is certainly the most efficient and least confusing method of spelling the sounds of Chinese words in the western alphabet.

A simple illustration of the variance between pinyin and the earlier Wade-Giles systems is apparent in the pronunciation of the capital of China – Beijing in pinyin and Peking in Wade-Giles.

Even in pinyin, there are some pronunciation traps to be overcome. For instance, Xi is pronounced Shi.

English is the major western language taught in China. With the development of its tourism industry, particularly in recent years, English-speakers will find their language spoken in major tourist facilities, particularly in joint-venture East-West hotels. Many staff have been trained in the west.

In the early days of these joint ventures, an amusing result was that hotel guests, who might pass through public areas many times within a short period as they went for breakfasts, arranged tours and met with friends, found they were being wished good morning and to have a nice day with incredible repetition by the same staff. It was a reverse of the old joke. Then, all western faces looked alike.

But Shanghai, with its colourful history of western trade, occupation and intervention, is the most westernised city in China and English is more widely spoken than anywhere.

A late afternoon or evening stroll along the lovely **Bund** in Shanghai will produce many approaches to the visitor in English. Congregating students like to practise the English they are learning at school or university.

Guides, staff of Friendship Stores and many upmarket shops speak English. Not all taxi drivers do.

INFOTIP: Always carry with you the business card of your hotel with its address in Mandarin so that if you do become lost, you can be returned safely to your Shanghai home.

The people of any nation appreciate the visitor who makes some effort to communicate in their own language. The Chinese are no exception and exhibit particular delight because they realise their languages are so difficult for westerners.

For any visitor intent on making anything but the most simple communication in Mandarin, a phrase book is an essential investment. For those who have not bought one in advance in their own country, there should be little difficulty in acquiring a phrase book in the shops which are part of all the major hotels in Shanghai and the other main Chinese cities.

A phrase book will indicate the four basic tones or accents needed to be placed on words. Naturally, they influence word meanings.

Here are a few helpful phrases.

Ni hao	Hello
Zaijian	Goodbye
Qing	Please
Xiexie	Thank you

Ni hao ma?	How do you do?
Xie xie ni, hen hao	I am well, thank you.
Wo yao dao...	I want to go to...
Wo yao mai...	I want to buy...
Shi	Yes
Bu	No
Duo shao qian?	How much is it?
Fei ji chang	Airport
Huo che zong zhan	Central railway station
You zeng ju	Post office
Ce suo	Toilet
Nan ren	Men
Nu ren	Women

yi	one
er	two
san	three
si	four
wu	five
liu	six
qi	seven
ba	eight
jiu	nine
shi	ten

From 11 to 19, numbers are formed by addition — eleven is ten plus one ie. shi-yi 11 and er-shi 20, er-shi-yi is 21.

Xiling Gorge

Chinese Mythology

Chinese mythology is a rich tapestry of folklore which, some scholars assert, can be traced in an almost clear line past the mists of pre-history to the neolithic period.

The myths of China that have become progressively stylised over the past two and a half thousand years appear to be little influenced by the mythology of other early civilisations but, like all primitive tribal societies, they represent attempts to trace their history to the beginning of time.

They speak of gods and demi-gods who ruled the world before the creation of the first man. **P'an Ku** who was the original mortal ruler of the world enjoyed supernatural powers.

He was followed by three emperors who, with snake bodies and human heads, ruled the Chinese race for tens of thousands of years.

The first prominent mortal emperor was **Sui Jen** who brought fire to man by producing sparks after watching a bird pecking at a tree.

A second mythological figure was **Fu Hsi** to whom is attributed the invention of marriage and of substituting a matriachal order to the human race over the previous patriachal society.

Fu Hsi is also credited with having taught hunting, fishing and animal husbandry to his people, with having invented musical instruments and supplanting an early form of knot-tying message communication with hieroglyphs. This legendary figure was also the inventor of the first calendar.

He was followed by the emperor **Shen Nung** who introduced agricultural implements, taught the tilling of fields to man and discovered the medicinal properties of plants.

Next in the Chinese mythological succession was the **Yellow Emperor, Huang Ti.** He refined the original calendar, built the first houses, created the first cities, brought order into commerce and trade and greatly extended the boundaries of his empire.

To his empress is attributed the first manufacture of silk thread and cloth.

Essentially, these Chinese folk heroes represent parallels with the creation and post-creation myths of the Australian Aborigines. Whether any such legendary figures existed is extremely doubtful, in the same context that Homer's Ulysses is a matter of historical debate although Chinese chronologies place these first three emperors' lives and achievements between 4000 and 3000 BC.

Huang Ti was succeeded by four other famous mythological emperors. Three of these, **Yao, Shun** and **Yu** were held up by Confucius as model rulers. There are a variety of dates attributed to their reigns and the reality of their existence is extremely uncertain.

The Chinese hold that Yu drained away the waters of a huge flood and founded the first dynasty in China. Yu's Hsia Dynasty came to an end with the reign of the tyrant emperor **Chieh Kuei** who was overthrown by the emperor **Tang,** founder of the Shang Dynasty which existed from 1765 to 1122 BC. It is at this point that mythology became supplanted by recorded history in China.

The existance of the **Shang Dynasty** and its rulers is beyond doubt and has been verified by a weight of archaeological discovery in recent times.

The Bund

Into this basic mythology is also entwined countless localised legends, some created by poets.

Visitors to Shanghai intending to cruise the mighty **Yangtze river** and pass through its beautiful Three Gorges may have the following story-legend recounted to them.

Two dark mountain peaks rise from the banks of the Yangtze near the famous **Qutang Gorge.** A local legend claims that 12 ferocious dragons were chasing each other around these mountains in play. Their flight created a great wind which blew down houses and killed thousands of people. At the time of this disaster, the **Goddess Yao Ji** who was the youngest daughter of the mythical **Mother of the Western Skies** passed by, riding on a brilliantly colored, floating cloud.

She pointed her finger at the dragons who were struck down by a resultant thunderbolt. They were turned into huge rocks that blocked the Yangtze river.

A local legendary hero **Yu the Great,** who already had a reputation for taming wayward rivers rushed to the scene and, with the help of the Goddess Yao Ji, he moved the huge boulders. But, the legend says, Yu and Yao Ji moved them to a wrong place and instead of the flood waters receding, the river rose higher and higher and they had to find another escape route for the water.

This narrow passage through enclosing mountains is the **Cuokai Gorge** which literally means the wrongly opened gorge.

前门宁道人民防空地道网

Empress Dowager

CHINESE DYNASTIES

Shang Dynasty

China's first historically provable dynasty –
Shang – is attributed to the years 1700 to 1100 BC. The dates are approximate. It was in this period that the first identifiable urban societies came into being.

The Chinese of the Shang period created bronze utensils of great beauty. The present Chinese system of writing was developed. Trade and commerce was carried on with cowrie shells as the means of exchange. The people had domesticated cattle, sheep, pigs, dogs and chickens.

Reverence of the family emerged. This was reinforced by ancestor-worship although other various spirits and gods were revered also.

It was a time of deep superstition and a system of foretelling the future came into vogue. This was achieved by heating bones and shells and then interpreting the cracks which appeared in them as they cooled.

The Shang Dynasty was brought to a close by the abuses of its last emperor, **Zhou Hsin** who was overthrown by the people on the western frontier of his domain.

Zhou Dynasty

The Zhou Dynasty combines the Western Zhou (1027-771 BC) and Eastern Zhou (770-256 BC.)

It was in this dynastic era that the majority of China's political infrastructure was created.

It was based on the concept that good and wise rulers received a mandate from heaven which, in turn, brought about the downfall of emperors who were cruel and corrupt. The disapproval of heaven on evil rulers was manifested in natural disasters such as flood and plague.

This judicial heaven also extended to the common people approval of the right to rebel against oppression and gave a mandate to the leaders of such rebellions to claim the throne.

In the Zhou period, although they were divided into hundreds of petty kingdoms, the Chinese people developed a spirit of shared identity. They believed in the superiority of their culture above all others and considered all other people from bordering lands to be barbarians.

Their culture was identified with a highly developed system of agriculture through irrigation. The dynasty marked the emergence of literature in the form of poetry and recorded history.

Schools were founded and commerce flourished between the separate kingdoms.

The Warring States

The period of the Warring States is generally attributed to 489 – 221 BC.

At the peak of the **Zhou Dynasty,** there were more than 1,700 relatively independent feudal kingdoms, the rulers of which acknowledged allegiance to the Royal House of Zhou.

As the power of the larger feudal states increased, the ability of the Zhou royalty to control them declined. The era of the Warring States was highlighted by continuous conflict which reduced the number of independent kingdoms to less than 200 and brought about extremes in poverty and wealth.

Confucius lived in this period and his philosophy of venerating good government was a natural result of the turmoil of his time.

In the middle of this era emerged a society based on the proliferation of land ownership as opposed to the feudal system in which all land was the property of the local ruler.

There is scholarly conjecture that this landlord class was created by conquering kings awarding areas of the defeated territories to their most outstanding soldiers in much the same way that Imperial Rome gave land to its long-serving legionnaires on their discharge from military service.

Another quite valid theory attributes the increasing individual land ownership to the freeing of feudal slaves following the defeat of their lords.

This system of landlords and tenant farmers continued into the next dynasty.

Qin Dynasty

The Qin Dynasty is one of the shortest in China's history (221 – 206 BC.)

But it was momentous because of the first unification of individual kingdoms into one empire.

Emperor Qin's swift military successes were accompanied by excesses of tyrannical rule. Like many despots who followed him, in both Chinese and western cultures, Qin destroyed all literature of the past which embodied ideas in conflict with those of his own. His brief reign was also marked by great public works in which the first sections of what became the **Great Wall of China** were created.

Roads were built to link his capital, which was located near the modern Chinese city of Xian, with the furthest outposts of his empire. These great advances were only achieved by the enforced labor of prisoners and peasants.

Qin also standardised systems of weight, measure and coinage throughout his empire. All were essential to the success of a centralised government.

On his death in 207 BC, the brutal excesses of his rule resulted in rebellion led by a common soldier **Liu Pang** whose army captured the capital.

Consistent with the concept of heaven's mandate being placed on the leaders of successful rebellions against oppressive rulers, Liu Pang declared himself emperor and became the first ruler of the Han Dynasty.

Han Dynasty

The Han Dynasty which extended from 206 BC to 220 AD encompassed two periods of power known as Former or Eastern Han and Latter or Western Han.

Former Han dated from 206 BC to 25 AD while Latter Han covered the period 25 BC to 220 AD.

None of the Han emperors ever achieved the complete power that Qin enjoyed.

They shared it with increasingly powerful regional officials whom they appointed, with rich provincial landlords and the wealthiest of families engaged in trade and commerce.

The reigns of the first four Han emperors were characterised by the progressive development of a highly ordered government bureaucratic system. The most important and influential of these positions were invariably held by the emperors' immediate families and loyal servants of the imperial courts.

Commencing in 147 BC, the **emperor Wu** embarked on a series of military incursions into neighboring lands which greatly expanded the boundaries of the Han empire. It was Wu who laid down a system of examinations for appointment to the public service which were based on the teachings of Confucius. This system continued as virtually the sole basis of education to the Chinese civil service for the following 2,000 years.

The emperor's military achievements to the west resulted in increasing contact with what were still considered the barbarian people of central Asia. Although this period of the Han Dynasty brought China's first contact with the western world and knowledge of the Roman empire in Europe and the Middle East, the tenuous linking with the cultures of India, the Middle East, Egypt, Greece and Rome had virtually no impact on the world of the Middle Kingdom.

Like those who had come before them, the emperors of the Han Dynasty faced the problem of foreign barbarians who, while culturally inferior to them, were militarily formidable and a constant threat to the frontiers of the empire. This resulted in a double-think style of diplomacy which forced the Han courts to treat the barbarian emmissaries as honoured guests although officially these were considered to be visits from inferior and subserviant people.

The expansion of the empire created the inevitable strains of distance and the emergence of provincial rulers leading armies necessary for the defence of their areas.

As the power of these regions increased, the inevitable resulted and, in 220 AD, the empire split into three contesting kingdoms.

While the concept of one unifying emperor remained, and there was always a ruler laying claim to being China's supreme leader, that person, whoever he was, lacked the power to enforce the claim.

The fragmenting of authority was an invitation to invasion by the nation's warlike neighbors, particularly in the north which, in this period, came under the sway of **Tobas**. These were Turkish-speaking tribes originating in central Asia.

A spin-off of this central Asian contact was the introduction of Buddhism by Indian merchants who were accompanied by Buddhist priests and, between the third and sixth centuries AD, Buddhism swept northern China.

But the conquering Tobas were eventually absorbed into the traditional Chinese culture, a phenomenon repeated nearly 1,000 years later after the Mongol incursion.

The Tobas as a distinct race ceased to exist.

In the south, the separate kingdoms which had emerged did not face the same problems of invasion.

Qin Dynasty Worrior

Tang Dynasty Tower

Sui Dynasty

In 589 AD, China was again unified, this time by a general of the northern kingdom and a descendent of the Toba invaders. He successively overwhelmed the southern kingdoms but his power was short-lived. In 618 AD, the infant dynasty was overthrown by another noble descended from both Chinese and Toba ancestors.

Tang Dynasty

The noble Tang family rapidly consolidated the unification of China and created a capital city close to modern **Xian.** This, at the height of its splendor, must have been the greatest metropolis in the world with a population of more than one million inside its formidable walls.

It was a glittering centre of Chinese culture and religion and a centre of world commerce, being the end point of the **Silk Road** from the west.

The Tang Dynasty held power until 907 AD and, even today, the period is regarded as the **Golden Age** of Chinese imperial power and wealth, a time of great creative advances in culture, learning and vast public works.

The Tang emperors increasingly became all powerful and this centralised power demanded efficient commmunication with the furthest outposts of their empire which, again, expanded to an area almost equal to that which China had enjoyed under the Han Dynasty.

The building of canals which had begun in the brief Sui Dynasty was vastly extended and a network of roads on which were a system of guest houses for imperial travellers and merchants was created.

This network of road and water transport connected the imperial capital with China's emerging sea ports to the east and the Asian caravan trails to the west.

The inevitable result was that China received the greatest influx of foreign influences in its history to that time and many of the religions of the west, including the Nestorian Christians based in Syria, established themselves in China along with zealous missionaries of Islam and Zoroastrians from Persia.

The efficiency of the Tang emperors' bureaucracy was a model that continued with successive dynasties for 1,000 years. But in the last decades of the eighth century, the military defeats by Turkish invaders from central Asia weakened the imperial power and the re-emergence of provincial war lords sounded the death knell of the dynasty which crumbled in 907 AD as China, once again, split into several kingdoms.

But the efficient trade links created by the **Tang emperors** remained and, economically, China continued to prosper until the nation was once again unified in 960 AD by a general of one of the southern states, **Chao K'uang-yin.**

Song Dynasty

The first Song emperor, who re-united China as much through diplomacy as military prowess, was able to maintain the prosperity inherited from the Tang era. China experienced two centuries of peace until, in the 12th century, the **Song court** was threatened by the so-called **Golden Tartars** with whom the Song Dynasty had allied itself to defeat a Mongol-speaking people, the **K'itan.**

The Tartars rapidly gained power over all of the empire north of the Yangtze River and the Song court fled to Hangzhou in the south where they quickly created a capital which, shortly afterwards, awed **Marco Polo** with its magnificent architecture and wealth.

But both the Tartar conquerors of northern China and the Song emperors to the south were about to be overwhelmed by an invasion, the fury of which has had few precedents in world history.

In the first decade of the 13th century, a Mongol prince, **Genghis Khan** had succeeded in uniting the nomadic Mongol tribes beyond the empire's frontiers. The Chinese had faced Mongols before and had always defeated them.

But the combined force of the Mongols was a threat never encountered before.

Yuan Dynasty

Genghis Khan's new Mongol nation broke through the Great Wall in 1213 and made short work of the Jin or Tartar regime.

The Mongols took Beijing two years after their invasion had commenced. The southern Song emperors enjoyed a brief respite while Genghis Khan turned back westward and campaigned successfully as far as Russia.

But the Mongols were in China to stay and the Song Dynasty was conquered by Genghis Khan's grandson, **Kublai Khan** in 1279.

He became the first emperor of the Yuan Dynasty and chose Beijing as his capital.

Kublai Khan further improved the imperial system of roads he had inherited from the Chinese and linked his empire with Europe along the path of conquest his grandfather had paved through Russia.

Although the Mongol empire in China initiated sweeping reforms like the Tobas before them, they had, culturally, little lasting effect other than a generation of European interest in the fabled empire of Cathay. The first authentic reports that the kingdoms of Europe received from Marco Polo were the stories of a Mongol-dominated China, a relatively short-lived era in the nation's long history.

Ming Dynasty

When Kublai Khan died in 1294, the ambitions of his Mongol regime began to deteriorate and, within 50 years, several rebel armies were contesting for dominance.

The Mongols fled Beijing when **Zhu Yuan-chang,** a man with humble origins, led his army in attack. This was after he had conquered most of southern China.

Altering his name to **Hong Wu** on self-proclamation as the Ming Dynasty's first emperor, he made Nanjing his capital for its southerly, less vulnerable position.

Taoism and **Buddhism** were installed as the religions of the State and the Tang Dynasty innovation of examinations through which officials would be selected was reinstated.

His empire was fairly prosperous but Hong Wu was a domineering ruler under whom the intellectual and the ambitious could not thrive as China became more isolated, in its economic independent and cultural arrogance, from the rest of the world.

Ming Tomb

Hung Wu's fourth son, **Yung Lo,** the third Ming emperor, transferred the capital to Beijing and was responsible for the temples and palaces which made the city one of the world's most outstanding architecturally. He also sent expeditions to many parts of the world.

Chinese culture was restored under later Ming rulers, There was artistic development, the novel emerged as a literary genre, libraries increased and also cotton was more widely cultivated along with crops from other lands.

European explorers, including Portugese who were ultimately expelled or killed, and missionaries arrived although St Frances Xavier had died while attempting to lead his Jesuits into the empire in 1552.

But the Ming Dynasty declined under limp leaderships and was overthrown by Manchu invaders from the north east in 1644.

Qing Dynasty

The Manchu invaders under one of their princes established the Qing Dynasty which, continuing until its demise in 1911, ranked as one of China's longest imperial houses.

Although the Ming Dynasty Chinese resisted stubbornly, all of the empire was effectively in Manchu hands by 1665. This consolidation of power again led to an expansion of China's frontiers and both Mongolia and Tibet quickly came under its domination.

The Qing emperors, while initially spurning existing Chinese culture and traditions, reacted like other Asian conquerors before them and

soon re-instituted the effient model of bureaucracy developed and refined by those who had ruled before.

Gradually, the Manchus were absorbed into the Chinese cultural traditions and, for this reason, China continued to be isolationist in its foreign policy, giving little heed to the fruits of the Renaissance in Europe and the start of the Industrial Revolution in the nations far to the west.

China had never been a maritime power of any significance. Strategically, its empire had always been defended on its western frontiers. There was no precedent for invasion from the sea and when Portuguese adventurers assisted in stamping out piracy in the coastal waters of southern China. the **Qing emperor,** possibly as a form of reward, allowed a trading enclave to be set up in Macau.

The wealth that Portugal reaped from this foothold in China was a swift source of envy to other European maritime nations and, by the middle of the 17th century, the Spanish, Dutch and British were all seeking their share of Chinese trade.

The Qing court first discouraged this foreign contact from the sea but in 1685, with the trade appearing to be in China's favor, opened **Canton** as a port for trade with Europe.

Britain, which had bought vast quantities of Chinese tea and silk, was at a loss to even the balance of trade and in the 1770s sought to solve this problem by selling opium, produced in India, to China.

With British encouragement, addiction to opium became rife to such an extent that in 1800, the Qing court banned the trade. The imperial decree had little effect on either the British and the Chinese merchants who were benefitting. Matters came to a head in 1839 when a huge store of opium was seized by the Chinese in Canton.

Britain's answer to the Qing government was to attack the city in the first of what developed into **four opium wars.**

In the third of the opium trade conflicts, France supported Britain militarily and both Russia and the United States sent naval assistance. The last opium war from 1859 to 1860 reinforced the reality of western military supremacy and each of the conflicts resulted in treaties which opened more of China's sea ports, including Shanghai, to European influences and gave westerners the freedom of travel anywhere in China.

Quite crushing war reparations were imposed on the imperial government and the Qing Dynasty was compelled to drastically reduce imperial customs' duties on European imports.

Literally, for the first time in its history, imperial China was forced to accept formal diplomatic ligations in its capital, Beijing then known to the west as Peking. Europeans and other foreigners could not be tried under Chinese laws.

Following the lead of the British, the French invaded and took **Kochin-China,** now part of Vietnam and the forces of the Russian Czar grabbed a large area of the Chinese empire in Siberia.

Effectively, Europe had compelled China to open its doors to the west by the end of the first half of the 19th century.

The weakening of imperial power inevitably led to discontent and then rebellion among the Chinese. In 1851, the **Taiping Rebellion** broke out and the movement soon controlled most of southern China with an army of more than one million, nearly half of whom were women.

Led by its founder, **Hong Xiuquan** who declared himself to be on a direct mission from the Christian god, the Taiping rebels went on a rampage of destruction of Buddhist, Confucion and Taoist temples. They captured Nanjing and seriously weakened Qing power by cutting off a large part of imperial taxation and revenue.

In many ways, the Taiping movement was enlightened, its policies including the abolition of slavery, polygamy, prostitution and arranged marriages. But the success of the Taiping Rebellion worried the western powers as much as it did the court in Peking.

Western diplomacy wisely preferred dealing with a weak Qing government riddled by corrupt bureacracy than zealous and almost puritanical, rebellious peasantry.

The British were quick to offer their assistance and the Empire struck back. The imperial armies, stiffened by disciplined British redcoats, and helped by highly trained mercenaries from Europe and America recruited by the emperor, quickly defeated the Taiping troops.

Nanjing was beseiged, captured and looted in 1864. There was horrendous slaughter of the defenders and Hong Xiuquan, by his own hand, entered the Heavenly Kingdom of Great Peace which he had been unable to establish on earth.

Foreign intrusion into China continued after the crushing of the rebellion but at a time when the nation needed a strong government as much as it had ever needed it in its long history, the child **emperor Guangxu** occupied the throne, having been placed on it at the age of six in 1861.

Imperial policy was made by his aunt, the dowager **empress Wu Cixi** who had risen from the rank of concubine. It was a policy based on the conservative past of the Qing Dynasty, resistant to any western innovation or modernisation. Over the next 50 years, her inward-looking policies were a blueprint for the final destruction of an imperial system that had had, with its ups and downs, ruled the Chinese people for nearly 3,000 years.

The policies did not bring peace. There was a war with France between 1883 and 1885, resulting in French annexation of Indo China and, with this precedent of a crumbling empire, Japan, Britain, Russia and Germany vied for spheres of trade and influence.

By the last years of the 19th century the United States was advocating a policy that would have allowed any foreign power to stake its claim to Chinese trade, bypassing the imperial government which, so ruinously in debt to the west, was compounding its problems with crushing taxation on the peasantry.

Western missionaries, protected by their governments, were free to evangelise every area of China, confusing traditional Chinese morality not only with the Christian religion but by the introduction of foreign education and social morals.

The dowager empress had, in the 1880s, made a belated attempt to modernise the nation from the point of view of defence. Despite the products of Chinese naval shipyards and arsenals, the Chinese imperial army was soundly defeated by the Japanese in the 1890s.

Yet Wu Cixi still distrusted the westernisation of China and undermined the attempts in 1898 by the emperor Guangxu to reform the government.

Imperial China was on the point of disintegration when a peasant-based uprising principally aimed against foreign influences as much as the Qing court broke out with incredible fury.

The **Boxer Rebellion** of 1899 was initially defeated by the imperial army and what had started out as an organisation opposed to the Manchus then allied itself with the government in a final desperate attempt to regain China for the Chinese.

The Boxers massacred Chinese Christians as enthusiastically as they killed Europeans. The Boxer army descended on the capital of Peking in 1900 and beseiged the fortified compound which housed all of the foreign embassies.

Although the Qing government declared war on Britain, France, Germany, Russia, Japan, Italy and the United States, the foreign legations troops managed to hold out against both the Boxers and the regular Chinese army.

The western allies formed a formidable relief force and, as it approached Peking, the Qing court fled far west to Xian. The Boxers, no match for modern forces, melted away. The Boxer leaders were caught and executed and some of the imperial officials suffered the same fate.

The western powers chose not to destroy the Qing Dynasty but, while finally reinforcing their joint supremacy over China, were content to maintain the dowager empress as the official ruler of the vastly weakened empire.

Wu Cixi realised too late that China could not survive in the 20th century by maintaining an education system and a bureaucracy based on the teachings of Confucius. But the last years of the Qing Dynasty were beset with problems that the dowager empress no longer had the power to solve.

Three years before she died in 1908, a number of covert organisations had merged under the leadership of a Cantonese intellectual, **Dr Sun Yat Sen** into an organisation calling itself **The Alliance for Chinese Revolution.**

China's last imperial emperor, **Puyi** was only two years old when he ascended his disintegrating throne.

In 1911, an army uprising broke out in the Yangtze river city of **Wuhan** and many other provincial leaders flocked to this rebel cause.

Within a few months, all of southern China had declared itself independent of the imperial government and in January 1912, the Chinese Republic was proclaimed with Dr Sun Yat Sen its first president.

Another face of China

The Republic of China

Based in Nanjing without a decent army, the republic had not the power of a former imperial army chief whose death ended his plan to become emperor in the north.

But before his death, **Yuan Shikai** had to accept ecomomic concessions from the Japanese who, during the first world war, threatened to reduce China to a Japanese colony after having taken over the German-occupied Shandong peninsula.

In this period of political chaos, large areas of China were controlled by local War Lords. Most had been generals in the last days of the Qing Dynasty. When Yuan Shikai died in 1916, many of his political opponents, who had fled China, returned. This resulted in an explosion of political and intellectual movements which, in Peking University, saw the foundation of the Chinese Communist Party under **Li Dazhao** and **Mao Tse Dong.**

The theories of Marxism spread to intellectual cells in many of China's cities. Following the Bolshevik Revolution in Russia, Soviet Comintern representatives encouraged these small groups to combine and the first congress of the Chinese Communist Party was held in Shanghai in July, 1921.

The Comintern advised the infant CCP to combine with the Nationalist or **Kuomintang Party** of **Dr Sun Yat Sen,** theorising on the Russian experience that a Marxist revolution in China could not be achieved before a general, national revolution was successful.

Dr Sun Yat Sen managed to control the CCP members of his party but when he died in Beijingin 1925, the unity began to dissolve as the political wing of the Kuomintang in which the communists wielded significant infuence and the Nationalist army of **General Chiang Kaishek** vied for supremacy in the movement.

Virtually a military government emerged, led by Chiang Kaishek who consolidated his power as the Nationalist Party leader when he married Dr Sun Yat Sen's sister .

Capitalism was preserved in China and the Communist Party turned its eyes to the countryside and the vast reservoir of Chinese peasantry to strengthen its hand. In the mid 1920s, the Nationalists made a determined effort to break the power of provincial War Lords and, with the help of a fifth column inside the city, the **National Revolutionary army** occupied Shanghai.

Chiang Kaishek seized the opportunity to wipe out the Communist movement in Shanghai and thousands of Shanghai CCP members were slaughtered. A name to loom large in the People's Republic of China, **Zhou Enlai** was one of the few in Shanghai to escape the massacre.

Within a year, Chiang Kaishek's army had taken Peking where Kuomintang government was established, controlling at least half of China, the rest still under the sway of local War Lords.

Following the Shanghai massacre, the CCP organised uprisings of peasants and workers in many areas of China and, despite very small armed forces, brought some parts of China under their control.

The policy of concentrating its efforts in the countryside paid off and by 1930, these small communist forces had swelled to an army of nearly 50,000. It defeated the Nationalists several times when Kuomintang forces were sent to destroy it.

But these initial successes did not last and when the **Red Army** changed its tactics from a guerilla style of warfare to a policy of fighting the Nationalist army head-on, it came close to total defeat. Retreat was the only answer to survival and, in October 1934, what remained of the communist forces began the famous **Long March** to the north, a journey of incredible hardship covering almost 8,000 kilometres and taking a year to complete.

All of this internal power struggle was occurring at the time when Japan was implementing its ambition to control China. The occupation of **Manchuria** had occurred in 1931. There, the last Qing emperor 'Puyi had been placed on the throne as a Japanese puppet ruler. Six years later, Japan invaded China proper.

By 1939, it had conquered roughly the whole of the eastern area of the country. Chiang Kaishek's government was forced to flee to Chongquing. The Nationalists took new heart when Japan attacked the United States on December 7,1941 and Chiang Kaishek continued a military policy of conserving his army, believing that with an inevitable American victory, he would need all of his forces to obliterate the communists.

For some time, the Nationalists had seen no need to form any alliance with the CCP even in the face of the invading Japanese. The Chinese Communist Party had used the war years to expand the Red Army and woo popular support far beyond the areas that they occupied.

When Japan surrendered, the Red Army numbered nearly one million and was prepared to face Chiang Kaishek's Nationalist forces in a struggle initially for Manchuria. The Red Army was victorious in several huge battles and there were mass desertions of Nationalist troops to the communist camp.

The Kuomintang deserters brought with them huge amounts of arms and equipment that had been supplied to Chiang Kaishek by the Americans. The final battle for the control of China was on.

From then on, the Red Army hardly knew even a minor defeat and, in October 1,1949, with Peking in communist hands, **Mao Tse Dong** proclaimed The People's Republic of China.

The last Nationalist resistence swiftly melted away and, with two million loyal soldiers and other Nationalist sympathisers, Chiang Kaishek fled to Taiwan under the protection of the United States which stubbornly refused to recognise the reality on the mainland.

The People's Republic of China

The first 40 years of the People's Republic of China was punctuated with great progress, disastrous set backs and, in the 1980s, by steady consolidation of its aims towards the goal of modernisation by the 21st century.

The central government led by **Mao Tse Dong** had inherited a China all but destroyed — a bankrupt country of chaotic road and rail communications and with agriculture and industry producing barely half the volume of the immediate pre-war years.

Inflation was rife but the new nation was united, particularly by the Korean conflict, to defend China from a perceived American invasion and the early 1950s was an era of incredible achievement. Gradually inflation was controlled through the nationalisation of all industry and the increase in agricultural production brought about by rural cooperatives which created a more efficient use of land.

The central government embarked on a grandiose scheme promulgated as the **Great Leap Forward.** It failed abyssmally and the disastrous policy was reinforced by flood, drought and the withdrawal of all Soviet aid which had helped the PRC to struggle through its first years.

The early 1960s were years of chronic food shortages and poverty although by 1965 the economy was gradually beginning to pick up.

Mao Tse Dong took much of the blame for the collapse of the Great Leap Forward and, politically, the star of his leadership waned. Under **Deng Xiao Ping** and **Liu Shauqi,** there was a return to family ownership of small land plots, free markets allowed and increase in agricultural production took precedence over both heavy and light industry.

The new direction could only succeed with a greatly expanded bureaucracy which was progressively created.

But Mao Tse Dong and his loyal follower **Lin Biao** still directly controlled the Red Army, a threat to any dramatic extensions of Deng's more liberal policies which Mao saw as the start of a return to capitalism and a betrayal of the revolution. The ageing leader decreed that China needed a cultural revolution to place it back in the right direction.

Late in 1966, the party's central committee adopted this policy. But this purist, Marxist line swiftly degenerated into the beginning of political and social chaos.

With his army backing, Mao Tse Dong got rid of any officials he feared opposed his will and, in 1967, even Liu was dismissed from his position and imprisoned as a traitor. Many other prominent party members simply disappeared.

A year earlier, the seeds of the disaster had come into full flower with the emergence of the **Red Guards,** a group that came into being in the Beijing University. Mao made an immense mistake in supporting and encouraging the expansion of this group. The Red Guards, with this initial patronage, rapidly became almost uncontrollable as teenaged students were incited to villify and attack their teachers and virtually any adult in a position of authority.

The Red Guards armed themselves and opposing units fought in a manner that threatened to come close to civil war.

Meanwhile, millions of discredited Chinese intellectuals, administrators and skilled tradespeople had been killed or banished to rural labor camps for 're-education.' The programme reached a point of insanity where even hotel chefs were relegated to dishwashing.

At the 11th hour, Mao Tse Dong called in the army to put an end to the Red Guards' actions, disarming them mostly by force.

The **Cultural Revolution** was also a period of cultural suppression hardly matched in history. Mao Tse Dong had reinforced his supreme leadership at terrible cost to national progress.

But he was growing old and at the National Congress of 1969, a new constitution believed to have been written by the leader nominated his old comrade Lin Biao to succeed him on his death.

Perhaps Lin was impatient because, just two years after the

Old Housing

Classical Pagoda

congress, Lin died in a plane crash while allegedly flying to the Soviet Union after a failed coup to topple Mao. The effective control of government now fell to **Zhou Enlai** who, in his position as premier, was loyal to the ageing Mao and, with what must have been the leader's concurrence, strengthened the central government structure and began overtures to the United States and other western nations for the expansion of trade and diplomatic contact.

This strategy resulted in president Richard Nixon's momentous visit to China in 1972.

Just one year later, the aftermath of the Cultural Revolution was laid to rest with the reinstatement of **Deng Xiao Ping** who, with **Zhou**

Enlai, instituted an era of increasingly moderate policies. Although the official cleansing of Deng could only have occurred with Mao Tse Dong's agreement, a power struggle emerged between the hard line Maoists and Zhou-Deng factions.

Mao's wife, **Giang Qing** was a prominent leader of the left wing faction and, when Zhou Enlai died in 1976, Deng also vanished from power amid official media reports that the PRC was again in danger of drifting into capitalism.

By 1976, Chairman Mao's health had deteriorated to a point where he was hardly seen for weeks at a time. The end came on September 9, 1976 less than two months after the disastrous northern Chinese earthquake which had been interpreted as a heavenly sign in much the same way as other natural catastrophes were believed to have preceded the collapse of great dynasties throughout Chinese history.

On Mao's death, his next nominated successor **Hua Guofeng** came to power and, within a month, ordered the arrest of Mao's widow and three other leaders of the leftist faction who were internationally labelled **The Gang of Four.** That supreme survivalist of the revolution Deng Xiao Ping emerged again from the political limbo in which he had rested and, in 1977, Deng became vice-chairman of the CCP and took the positions of vice-premier and head of the People's Liberation Army.

Deng's return resulted in yet another power struggle with Hua Guofeng who managed to retain his leader's position until September 1980 when he acknowledged the inevitable and handed the premiership to a respected party functionary, **Zhao Ziyang.** Deng's ascendency was reinforced in 1981 when his long-standing protege **Hu Yaobang** supplanted Hua Guofeng as chairman of the party.

With no outstandingly surpreme leadership, the People's Republic of China was now effectively directed by the **Standing Committee** of the Communist Party whose six members included Hu Deng and Zhao.

The highly publicised trial of the Gang of Four acted out its foregone conclusion and, although Mao's widow received the death sentence, this was eventually commuted to life imprisonment. Another member of the Gang, Zhang Chunqiao similarly escaped execution. Their two fellow conspirators had received long prison sentences at the trial's end.

In the early 1980s, Deng and his allies neutralised the left faction by denouncing and gaoling any of Mao's supporters who represented even a mildly significant threat. The purge continued until the mid 1980s, a consolidation of power which, though neither vindictive nor violent, resulted in millions of communist party members being expelled.

Under Deng's leadership, many relatively youthful and previously hardly-known party members were appointed to important government and CPP positions.

As the People's Republic of China entered the last decade of its first 50 years, there appeared every prospect of an on-going stability in the central government and liberalisations both internal and external.

China original isolationist philosophy appeared to be firmly buried and its exploding tourism industry was a significant though relatively minor example of the country's understanding that its goals of modernisation would be more quickly and better achieved through cooperation with the developed nations in the capitalist world.

PART II
Sightseeing

SHANGHAI, THE PARIS OF THE EAST

Once notorious — for vice, corruption, good times, wild rumbustious days and the epitome of western elegance and decadence combined with the most abject poverty and squalor of the people — Shanghai is one of the world's most colourful cities and one of its largest.

Fifth largest city on earth, Shanghai is China's most populous with more than 12 million residents and is the country's biggest urban centre. It is located midway along China's east coast. The **Yangtze River** estuary flowing from west to east is less than 30 kilometres from the centre of Shanghai and the **Huangpu River,** which links Shanghai with the Yangtze, connects the city with the Pacific ocean and the inland cities of Nanjing, Wuhan and Chongqing.

Via the Suzhou Creek, which is a common name for the **Wusong River,** Shanghai is also connected to the **Grand Canal.** With part of its neighbouring provinces of Jiangsu and Zhejiang, Shanghai lies on the Yangtze delta which has flat ground, fertile soil, plenty of rain and a moderate climate. This makes it, economically, one of the richest agricultural regions of China.

While it is regarded as China's leading commercial centre, its provincial neighbours are challenging it because of greater economic reforms which have taken place during recent years. Centre of the Shanghai Economic Zone, which includes the above provinces, plus that of Jiangxi, Shanghai is one of 14 open coastal cities in China.

The name, Shanghai, translates literally as 'up from the sea.'

With an area of more than 6000 square kilometres, the municipality of Shanghai is divided into seven rural districts and 14 urban areas. In the latter, around 230 square kilometres, about seven million people are concentrated. Hence the newly-arrived visitor gains an overwhelming impression of high-density living and crowds everywhere in the downtown area.

An impression of modern, western sophistication is also given by the proliferation of contemporary, western-style buildings — luxury hotels and high rise steel and glass office complexes. These contrast with once grand mansions, reflections of the elegant lifestyles of resident westerners, and wide, tree-lined boulevards which, from the 1920's earned Shanghai the title of The Paris of the East. As charming as this reference was, Shanghai was also known as The Whore of China.

The most romantic manner to arrive in Shanghai is by steamer on the river which places into odd perspective teeming life on the water in China's main port with a skyline which leaps from the 1920s to the 1980s.

But probably most visitors to Shanghai will arrive via the main, newly renovated international and domestic Hongqiao Airport on the outskirts of the city. The airport, one of four in Shanghai municipality, is regarded as China's best. Southern Guangzhou and northern Beijing are about two hours flying time away. Tourists arriving by train will discover the central railway station is in the north central part of Shanghai.

Several cruise lines, including Pearl Cruises, Royal Viking Line and CTC Cruises, include Shanghai on China/Asia intineraries. Visitors can also elect to leave Shanghai by ship to Hong Kong or take a slow boat in China by sailing to Wuhan, Chongqing, Ningbo, Fuzhou, Dalian, Qingdao and Wenzhou.

History

In comparison with much of China, Shanghai's history is relatively unspectacular. It was said to have risen from the sea 5000 years ago. Up to the 19th century, it existed as a port which relied on trade and fishing for its existance.

Shanghai played no part in the turbulent establishment of the Chinese Empire until the coming of the British in the 19th century. For this reason, its past is rarely retraced in publications written for tourists. Yet its earlier history leading up to its days of danger and dalliance is worthy of inclusion for the interest of visitors.

In about the 6th century BC, the area that is now Shanghai was part of the **State of Wu.** In the early Warring States era, commencing in 480 BC, it was subservient to the **State of Yue.** It then became a possession of Prime Minister **Huang Xie** of Chun Shen of the **State of Chu.** Shanghai became known as **Shen** for short.

After China's unification by the Qin Dynasty's first Emperor, the area came under the **Huiji** prefecture. Suzhou to the north, was the seat of government. In the second century BC salt works were established. In the 3rd century AD, the present area of Shanghai was turned into a naval base by the commander in chief of the **Kingdom of Wu.**

Following the Eastern Jin Dynasty's transfer of China's capital to **Nanjing** in the 5th century AD, the civilization which expanded from the central plains of China soon touched areas south of the Yangtze River. It was at this time that a significant fishing industry developed in the Shanghai region.

In the 7th century, the Sui Dynasty emperor, **Yangdi,** forced millions of workers to gouge out the 2000 kilometre-long Grand Canal which linked communications enabling Shanghai to grow both economically and culturally.

In 751 AD, the Tang Dynasty established an administrative area to

the north of present day Shanghai and created a port at the existing settlement of **Qinglong**. It soon became a major trading centre on the south-eastern coast of China.

From the 10th to the 13th centuries, the small town of Qinglong was a secluded haven for many famous writers and painters of the Song Dynasty who left behind them a treasure trove of art.

By the middle of the 13th century, the lower reaches of the Wusong river were beginning to silt up and ships could no longer reach Qinglong and were forced to sail further south to the junction of the Huangpu River and Suzhou Creek, dropping anchor in an area known as **Shanghaipu.**

This is now that section of the Huangpu River on which the famous **Bund** is situated. The small township of Shanghaipu began to flourish as a centre of maritime commerce. Shanghaipu quickly supplanted Qinglong as a port for domestic and foreign trade.

By the end of the 13th century, the Yuan Dynasty had defined a Shanghai administrative district. The cultivation of cotton was begun and quickly expanded and, in the first years of the Ming Dynasty, Shanghai emerged as the largest textile centre in China. By the end of the Ming Dynasty, about 70 per cent of all of the rural land around Shanghai was planted with cotton to supply the increasing needs of the city's cotton-spinning industry which, by the middle of the 18th century, had created work for more than 20,000 citizens.

Although Japanese diplomats had arrived by sea during the Tang Dynasty on their way to Xian, it became necessary to defend the city against Japanese pirates during the period of the Ming Dynasty which fortified the city's ramparts.

In 1685, the Qing Dynasty chose Shanghai as the major customs centre for trade along the Yangtze River.

Shanghai continued to grow and, by the mid-19th century, was a bustling port. This was due also to the fact that silk production had developed and increased in Shanghai's surrounding regions and the port was a natural outlet to foreign markets.

The Huangpu River was a forest of masts of the ships of the maritime nations of the world.

The dramatic change from a mainly agricultural economy occurred after China suffered a humiliating defeat by Britain in 1842 – the first opium war.

China had surrendered Shanghai and under the terms of the **Treaty of Nanking,** the city was open to unrestricted foreign trade. Beside the British, France and the United States occupied their own areas of the city in which they enjoyed total privilege. But the Shanghai Chinese found themselves outcasts in certain areas of their own city.

In 1895, Japan also received a concession in Shanghai with the signing of the **Treaty of Shimonoseki.**

The opening of Shanghai to world trade saw major western banks and the large commercial businesses of Europe and America establish branches in the city and Shanghai's emergence as the premier foreign port of China was further advanced during the **Taiping Rebellion** between 1850 and 1864. This uprising cut off the other major western concessional port of Canton from the trading products of southern China. The rebellion which limited Britain's goals of expansion and resulted in Britain forcing navigation rights on the Yangtze River in 1857.

Shanghai was the natural outlet for the huge Yangtze basin and, by 1860, more than a quarter of all foreign ships trading with China docked in Shanghai.

The city still did not emerge as a significant industrial centre until the 1890s although the Qing Dynasty had established its main military arsenal there 50 years earlier.

Small manufacturing businesses that existed there before the 1890s supplied the immediate needs of the big foreign trading establishments.

This began to change following the Sino-Japanese war of 1894-95 when an increasing number of light manufacturing businesses were established in all of the foreign concessions.

The Chinese took little part in this early industrialisation of Shanghai and it was not until the years of the first world war that local Chinese investors were able to participate in the development of an industrial economy in their city.

These first Chinese financed industries in Shanghai were mostly overwhelmed by a resurgence of western and Japanese economic imperialism in the 1920s and the Depression in the 1930s.

Conditions for the Chinese people generally were horrendous as their living conditions had progressively deteriorated into filthy slums while the foreigners continued to live the high life in buildings they had modelled on the architectural styles popular in their homelands.

Even before the outbreak of the Sino-Japanese war in 1937, Japanese businesses controlled more than half of Shanghai's yarn-spinning and weaving production.

An offshoot of this exploitation was the birth of modern political awareness by the Chinese in Shanghai. The workers, as well as students and intellectuals, became more involved in the search for a political solution to this foreign oppression and, when the western powers failed to fulfill demands against the dumping of cheap foreign goods on the Shanghai market (which had been agreed to at a conference in Washington in 1922,) the Chinese retaliated by imposing boycotts on these imports.

The first massive demonstration against western economic imperialism came in 1925. This was the May 30 uprising of students and workers in Shanghai led by the Chinese Communist Party which had been founded in the city in 1921. This huge demonstration of political frustration was aimed as much against Chinese official involvement in foreign imperialistic ventures as it was against capitalism.

This first coalition between workers and students supported **Chiang Kaishek** who repaid this support by ruthlessly suppressing armed uprisings between October 1926 and March, 1927.

Very few leading members of the CCP in Shanghai escaped the massacres by the Nationalist army.

In the 1930s, Shanghai's world reputation as an adventurer's paradise rose to its zenith. While the servants of foreign millionaires draped their limosines with furs so the motors would function after winter evenings of feasting in glittering surroundings, Chinese beggars, paupers, the sick and deformed lay dead in the gutters nearby from starvation, illness and exposure.

Surviving Shanghaiese were burdened beasts; many of their children sold into slave labor.

And beneath the blatant,contrasting surfaces of Shanghai's polarised fortunes of foreigners and the local, downtrodden poor was a teeming, seemy other life of sailors and swindlers, socialites and sinners on every scale seeking the thrills that came of drug running and addiction, gambling, over-indulgence in food and drink at the grandest of establishments, prostitution, stealing and survival by wits.

Shanghai was occupied by Japan soon after that country invaded China in 1937. The city remained in Japanese hands until the end of world war two in 1945 and Shanghai's pre-ward industry was badly damaged during the period although foreigners maintained their lifestyles until the west declareds war in 1941. Then they were interned by the Japanese.

Between the end of world war two and the fall of Shanghai to the **People's Liberation** in 1949, foreign powers relinquished their territorial concessions in Shanghai to the **Nationalist government.** The economic chaos worsened with inflation reaching proportions equalling that of Germany immediately after world war one.

There was no plan of reconstruction and, while the general population faced semi-starvation, many Nationalist politicians and their business partners flourished by exploiting even further the misery of Shanghai.

Perhaps more so in Shanghai than in any city of China, the soldiers of the People's Liberation Army were welcomed of the saviors of the city when they entered it on May 26, 1949.

Once in control, the CCP set about the massive task of turning this ruined cesspool of the world into a window on to China's plans for dramatic progress and modernisation.

Drug addicts and prostitutes in their thousands were rehabilitated through enforced employment and pimps and dealers who had exploited them were mostly executed.

The city which had once been notorious for its gambling halls catering to the Chinese and the famous race course exclusively for the indulgence of the foreign population were eliminated.

The first years of the 1950s marked emerging prosperity fuelled by the uncrushed, optimistic industry of its people. Like the rest of the People's Republic, Shanghai's development slowed down during the economic failure of the **Great Leap Forward.** That plan, which placed emphasis on the swift development of heavy industries to the detriment of agricultural production result in serious food shortages in Shanghai up until 1960, although the city suffered less in this regard than other major centres in China.

Shanghai had only begun to emerge again as China's major manufacturing and scientific centre when it was hit by the dark decade of the **Cultural Revolution.**

In fact, Shanghai played a leading role in this Great Leap Backwards as Mao Tse Dong's wife, **Jiang Qing** and many of her closest political allies were the city's major proponents of the Revolution's extreme left wing philosophies. The excesses of the Red Guards were notorious in Shanghai and the city's life blood for the future – its students, artistans, trained industrial workers and intellectuals were banished to the countryside. Of the estimated 500,000 expelled from the city during the Cultural Revolution, the majority have never returned.

The favored place for their exile and 're-education' was the far western province of **Xinjiang** where an estimated 50,000 Chinese representing Shanghai's most promising students at the start of the Cultural Revolution still remain.

By the end of the 1980s, China largest city again boasted the biggest pool of the nation's technical expertise. Shanghai is the centre for about 15 per cent of the PRC's industrial production while a fifth of all the nation's exports pass through the port.

Significant foreign investment has returned to Shanghai although great western multi-national corporations that have established there in recent years refer to the city's leftist local politics as a continuing problem.

Shanghai began to regain its pre world war two importance as a great financial centre when, in 1986, the Stock Exchange, which had once flourished, was re-opened.

In the same year, the Shanghai **Municipal Government** announced more enlightened regulations relating to foreign trade in an attempt, not only to induce increased foreign investment in the development of the city but also aimed at convincing those potential investors that their contracts and their profits would be safe.

Although the hospitality industry was the first to benefit from these policies, with the construction of joint-venture Western hotels, there has been a swing away from the tourist industry towards the encouragement of foreign investment in industry which covers a spectrum embracing iron and steel production, heavy machinery, chemicals, motor vehicles, electrical equipment, shipbuilding, paper manufacturing and printing to name but a few.

This does not mean that Shanghai has ceased to develop facilities for tourists and business-people who have come to expect the highest standards of accommodation, cuisine, entertainments and communications available in China.

In 1989, the international Peninsula Hotels' group was supervising the construction of a new luxury hotel the Shanghai Portman while the Shanghai Mandarin was being built for the Mandarin Hotels' chain. Several other promiment international hotel chains, principally Holiday Inns, Novotel, New World Hotels and Sara Hotels were also either commencing construction of or finalising negotiations for new hotel projects in Shanghai.

Where, a decade before, the city could not cope with the demands of western tour operators and visiting business people, Shanghai may, by the mid 1990s be plagued with a competitive situation of too many first class and luxury beds.

Although Shanghai is a vast, expanded city, its main streets follow a regular criss-cross pattern. There are numerous landmarks which the first-time visitor will soon recognise.

A network of trolley buses transverses much of Shanghai and maps displayed on the back, front and sides of the buses indicate routes by numbers. The trolley buses are not expensive and run frequently but they are invariably crowded.

Do not bet or even hope to hail a taxi on the street. They are available outside most hotels. If not, ask the porter to arrange one for you.

INFOTIP: While many taxis are metered, many drivers will not use the meters. Negotiate the fare (which will be dependent on the driver and whether or not traffic is busy at that time of day.) This negotiation should take place in front of the hotel so that staff can interpret should language be a problem – and it usually is!

If you are daring, you can hire small three-wheeled motor cycles such as used by locals but their safety is not guaranteed. Otherwise, hire a bicycle very cheaply ... but once you see the crowds and the traffic, you may be deterred.

Yangtze River

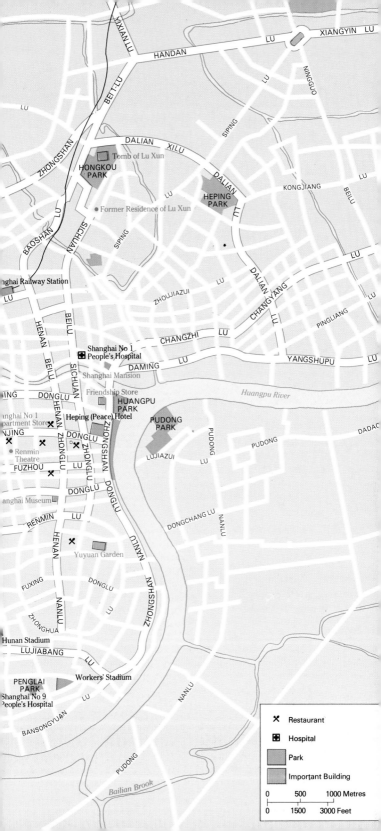

The Bund

To anyone who has investigated and walked the great avenues and boulevards of the world, The Bund of Shanghai needs no introduction. It is as the Champs-Elysees of Paris, London's Park Lane, New York's Madison Avenue and the Via Veneto of Rome, except it has a unique, waterfront aspect.

If the visitor to Shanghai is limited in time, The Bund is the place to feel the throb of the city's heart and to be reminded of its glorious and inglorious past.

The Bund is a wide and gracious avenue which lines the western bank of the **Huangpu River** near where it is met by the Suzhou Creek. It is a romantic-sounding name which many believe has German derivation. But The Bund is actually Anglo-Indian for a muddy, waterfront embankment. It was originally a muddy tow-path known as **Waitan** by the Chinese. The Bund was appropriately named for the time between 1920 and 1965 when Shanghai sank in a manner similar to the problem of Venice.

Against this remaining threat, foundations of concrete are used to support any building in an area where the problem could occur again.

The Bund became the focal point of Shanghai after European occupation. It is now known as **Zhongshan Dong Yi Lu,** and remains a classic reminder, with its impressive European architecture, of the city's grandeur under foreign influence.

Early in the morning, visitors will see spontaneous exhibitions of **tai chi,** a form of disciplined and somewhat poetic exercise practised by Chinese country-wide, particularly in places of aesthetic inspiration, such as parks or areas adjoining water.

> **INFOTIP:** Visitors are welcome to join the Chinese in their exercises, and also those which take place at Huangpu Park which is just opposite the Shanghai Friendship Store a short distance from the waterfront.

For the rest of the day, entertainment on The Bund is in watching the Shanghaiese and visitors stroll, walking through free markets from which one can buy commodities ranging from pornography to clothing, typical Shanghai snack foods and cheap toys. The promenade becomes a lovers' lane by evening but there are still people wishing to converse in English with those who would share with the citizens the romantic night atmosphere of Shanghai's former 'Wall Street' from the time it was dominated by the western powers.

While the buildings maintain the exteriors which reflect neo-classical styles of New York and Chicago plus a few unexpected variations on Egyptian achitecture, inside, their functions as commercial and apartment buildings, hotels, banks and clubs have altered.

One hotel can be regarded as perhaps Shanghai's most famous landmark. The green-towered **Peace Hotel** consists of two buildings. The north and south buildings are on opposite corners of busy Nanjing Road where it joins The Bund. Built in 1929, the north building was originally The Cathay Hotel which was regarded as the most luxurious and best hotel in all of the Far East. The other building is the former Hui Zhong Hotel built in 1906. Both wings have been renovated and have huge suites and enormous bathrooms. The Peace Hotel suites

Special Handicrafts

are each decorated in a different theme reflecting nine countries. These are China, England, the United States, France, Germany, India, Spain, Italy and Japan. The restaurants also reflect the days of foreign consessions, and retain their turn-of-the-century atmosphere.

The British country pub atmosphere is still found in the cocktail lounge with its renowned Peace jazz combo. Service is not bad and suites are clean.

After strolling The Bund or shopping in Nanjing Road, drop in for a drink in this ageing memorial to the colonial days of the British Empire and imagine how good the white-garbed civil servants, merchants and soldiers had it in the 1930s.

Authentic Shanghai dishes are served there and in the north wing, there is an excellent ground floor bookshop for browsing and buying publications which you may not find anywhere else in Shanghai – or China, for that matter.

Another hotel which has a fantastic view of the Huangpo River, Suzhou Creek and The Bund is The **Shanghai Mansions.** It has gone to seed a bit but the location for a coffee, drink or meal is fine. Best view of the river looking across to where the Hunagpu meets the Wusong is from the rooftop terrace. If you are staying, be warned that the horns of the river boats may keep you awake. They were noisy enough for Mao's wife, Jiang Qing to prohibit traffic moving on the river when she was overnighting in Shanghai.

The branch offices for **China's Foreign Trade Corporation** are based in four buildings adjacent to the Bank of China. Once, Japanese and American banks used the buildings. The former Hong Kong and

Shanghai Bank, a huge granite edifice circa 1929, is home to the Shanghai **People's Municipal Government.** The building, which used to house the Royal Air Force Club, is now off limits to visitors.

Erected in 1927, the Customs House still functions as such. Up till recently, the Anthem of the Cultural Revolution — The East Is Red — used to be chimed out from the Customs House clock tower.

Police now carry out their duties in the former American Club.

The **Huangpu Park,** where visitors can join locals in morning exercises, is at the north-west end of The Bund. During western occupation, Chinese and dogs were banned from the park which was then the British Public Gardens. It was here during the Boxer Rebellion of 1900 that the English posted a force from the Indian Army to protect themselves.

The park is a peaceful place in which to observe the ever-changing scene on the river from beneath shady trees. There are delightful flower beds and rock gardens.

You can visit the former Shanghai Club which was a oh-so-very exclusive establishment for upper class Englishmen. It is now the **Dong Feng Hotel.**

One of the best ways to get a perspective of the skyline of The Bund, is to take a Huangpu River trip on one of several large pleasure boats, which leave from moorings a few hundred metres north of the start of Nanjing Road. The trips which usually go to the junction with the Yangtze River and on to Wusongkou, last nearly four hours. There are afternoon and evening departures and, on the return section of the trip, passengers can usually see a performance of Chinese acrobatics and conjuring on one of the lower decks.

Alternatively somewhat violent kung fu videos may be offered.

Western tourists are generally segregated from the locals who also find the 60 kilometre return voyage on the river an attractive outing. The two largest of these river ships both have small souvenir shops and there are bars and snack foods on offer.

Once past The Bund proper, the views of the river banks are not so inspiring. Photography is effectively banned because the Huangpu River appears to be the anchorage for a sizeable portion of what passes for a navy in the People's Republic of China. But the life and commerce of the river is fascinating. The occasional junk in full sail and many fragile sampans can inspire the imagination of what water activity was like in the 1920s. But you will no longer see poor coolies loading and unloading the 15,000 river steamers and about 2000 sea-going vessels which bring or transport cargo to or from Shanghai every year.

> **INFOTIP:** Once aboard one of these cruise vessels, stake your claim to a reasonably comfortable deck chair on the sheltered stern of the main deck. The windows of the enclosed areas are frequently grubby, restricting both observation and photography, while the speed of the ships — about 18 knots on average — tends to make the deck areas near the bow uncomfortably windy, particularly in the late autumn, winter and early spring.

Tickets can be bought in advance from China International Travel Service's office at The Peace Hotel or on the dock.

Exploring Nanjing Road

Shanghai is the largest shopping centre in China. It has more than 40,000 individual shops and stores, thousands of which line Nanjing Road or occupy upper floors of the buildings along it.

Known as Nanjing Lu, the street stretches about 10 kilometres from The Bund to Jiangsu Lu. There are also many theatres, cinemas and restaurants along the city's most frenetic thoroughfare. Now, the Shanghai visitor will not see as many coffin makers located on Nanjing Road as there were in the rip-roaring, but also tragic days of death before 1949.

Nanjing Road east, or Nanjing Donglu, extends from the Peace Hotel to the Park Hotel. This section of less than two kilometres is the Oxford Street of the People's Republic of China. But the whole thoroughfare is so crowded that the unprepared visitor will be astounded at a concentration of humanity, which, when walking against it, is like meeting a continuous, breaking wave of people.

> **INFOTIP:** If you are shopping, or just walking to window-shop with more than one friend, specify a time later and a place with which you are familiar to meet. It is very easy to be separated from companions and literally 'drowned' in this ocean of people jamming the sidewalks and the roadway itself.

Let us take a stroll roughly west from the river to The Park Hotel. From the Peace Hotel's north wing – that's the right hand side of the road – you will soon be upon The Shanghai **Handicraft Exhibition Centre.** Built in the classic style of the Russians in 1955 – sometimes referred to as a 'Stalinist Stinker' – the former Palace Of Sino-Soviet Friendship is dominated by a high, steel spire, crowned with a nightly illuminated Red Star. Its massive halls are decorated in a heavy baroque style and it has a permanent exhibition of industrial products covering about 4000 individual items.

These include machinery, medical equipment, digital watches and clocks. There is a big display of Shanghai Municipality's arts and crafts and, because it sells thousands of top-quality products from antiques to silk garments and jewellry, it is inevitably included on a serious shopper's itinerary. The centre also houses on its highest floor quite a good Cantonese restaurant where prices are reasonable.

There are several other restaurants just along from the Handicraft Exhibition Centre including the Yangzhou Restaurant at number 308 which supplies distinctive Yangtze River dishes to groups of a minimum of eight. If you are not seeking a full meal, you could try the Guangming Tea Shop just a few doors down.

There is an interesting painting and calligraphy shop – Douyunxuan – just across the intersecting Shanxi Lu at 422. It stocks a better variety of prints and scrolls than the Shanghai Friendship Store or the Number One Department Store. Further west is one of the many beauty salons, the Xinxin, which have restored the art of hair dressing to not only Nanjing Road, but to China. During the Cultural Revolution, this art was condemned for its western decadence.

> **INFOTIP:** Western women, particularly with curly hair which is not as the hair of the Chinese, should describe the manner in which they expect their hair to be styled. Otherwise an enthusiatic assistant might spend hours trying to get the westerner's natural curls to lay flat, Chinese style.

The most fashionable shop in the whole length of Nanjing Road to buy silks of various weights and colours, cotton fabrics and ready-to-wear clothes – is the Shanghai Silk Store at 592. For those interested in Chinese herbal cures, the Shanghai No 1 Medicine Store is just a few steps further. On the same side of the road is the No 1 Food Store which is fascinating to browse in, if not to buy. Then comes the No 1 Department Store at 830.

As it serves about 100,000 shoppers daily, double this number on public holidays, be prepared to queue for your choice of about 37,000 individual products displayed in its many departments.

In the next block is the Overseas Chinese Hotel (104 Nanjing Xilu) with its red star-topped clock tower. Step inside to see its lavish foyer or try its Fujianese food.

Street Vendor

At number 170 is the Park Hotel built in 1934. It is one of Shanghai's landmarks and its restaurants are popular with visitors. One features banquets, including Peking Duck but these must bs ordered ahead. In Shanghai's halycon days, part of the roof of the top storey could be slid back, enabling wealthy diners to eat by starlight. The Park overlooks the Renmin Square and Renmin Park, the former racecourse.

Known as **People's Park** and People's Square, this area covers a square mile. Originally the area was traced out by a foreign horseman with his sword point. In 1861, he acquired all farms and buildings which were within the oval he had marked out. Now, the grassed park has ponds and shaded paths. There is also a museum with bronze, jade and ceramics. Centuries ago, tortoise shells were heated to encourage cracking by which the future was predicted. There are some of these tortoise shell artifacts on display.

One of the oldest buildings in Shanghai is its **Municipal Library**. Adjacent to the park, it is the former racecourse clubhouse.

The square is 35 hectares and a venue for political meetings and celebrations. It was here in April, 1969 that more than 2.5 million people gathered to protest against the Russians after frontier incidents with the People's Liberation Army.

If you deviate west of the park off Fuzhou Road, you will find yourself in the notorious **Blood Alley** where about 1.2 million opium addicts comprising 20 per cent of the city's population hung out in the years before 1949. The area was then the most infamous red light district in the Far East. More than 1000 prostitutes worked the district. In just one street known as 'Meet-With-Happiness Lane,' more than 30 exclusive bordellos functioned. Renamed **Liberation Lane,** the narrow street is still inhabited by some aged former ladies of the night.

The little restaurants which border Fuzhou Lu are former tea houses which were really just fronts for the world's oldest trade. It is a fascinating street to walk and you will also find interesting book shops.

Before crossing Nanjing Xilu to Renmin Park, you might like to walk west as far as Chengdu Lu. On the right hand side you will pass the Shanghai Arts and Crafts Store at 190. The third level is reserved for foreign shoppers only. Next comes the Renmin (or People's) Restaurant at 226. It specialises in dishes from the city of Suxhou and Wuxi. Then you will discover the **Acrobatic Theatre.**

This is China's first modern acrobatics and circus theatre. It has a circular stage and evening shows include performing giant pandas, monkeys, tigers, dogs and also highly skilled performers of traditional circus acts, clowns etc. The amphitheatre at number 400 Nanjing Xilu was built especially for acrobatic acts in 1981. Open every night except Tuesday. It is an absolute must for the visitor.

Not much further down is the Shanghai Plants and Bird Shop where you will find fresh flowers for sale. If this seems a surprising revelation, it is because the people of Shanghai prefer plastic flowers in their cramped appartments so the Real McCoy is relatively hard to find in the city. There are also bonsai among other plants, caged birds and exotic fish.

This is a natural point to begin retracing your steps eastward towards The Bund on the opposite side of the road.

There are many noteable restaurants on this side of Nanjing Road including the Xinya at 719 which offers a good Cantonese menu, and the Szechuan at 457 specialising in that province's traditional spicy to fiery dishes. To fuel your walk, there are snack stalls and cake and Chinese confectionary shops galore and, there,the locals will be as interested in watching you as you will be in observing them.

At number 345 is the biggest book shop in Shanghai, the Xinhua Bookstore. If you do not want to buy the book, you can hire it, as the store also operates as a kind of commercial lending library. Then stroll on to 309 if you are interested in Chinese flags, banners and home decorations at the Signs and Banners Store.

Things to consider buying along Nanjing Road (and other major shopping areas, including Szechuan Beilu,Jinling Donglu, Huaiahi Zhonglu, the Friendship Store on Beijing Donglu and the old quarters of the city) include embroidered fabrics, silks of course,padded winter jackets, shoes, woollen goods, painted fans, carved chopsticks, scroll paintings, brushes and calligraphy equipment, stationery, traditional musical instruments and carved stone seals.

The Friendship Store

Throughout China the Friendship Stores are inevitably regarded by tourists as attractions and indeed, if one does not have sufficient time to browse and compete with the crowds, these stores offer one-stop shopping at fixed prices with the bonus that many staff speak English.

Like the other Friendship Stores in China, Shanghai's accepts major credit cards, and has money-changing facilities.

INFOTIP: Outside the Friendship Store or your hotel, you may be approached to exchange money on the black market. You will have been issued Foreign Exchange Certificates (FEC in yuan) on arrival in China. The locals deal in renminbi which you should try to avoid receiving as change when shopping in stores other than those with sections for foreigners. Black market exchange is illegal and renminbi notes cannot be re-exchanged for western currencies or used in major hotels, most restaurants many taxis, etc. If you are stuck with change in renminbi, you can spend it in shops patronised purely by the Chinese.

Landscape from Longua

Shanghai's Friendship Store has moved from its original location in the British Consulate building on The Bund to 40 Beijing Donglu close to the Peace Hotel.

It sells literally everything the westerner wants to buy in China – the products mentioned previously plus gems and pearls, jade, ivory, antiques, curios, vases, imitation bronzes, furniture including redwood screens and reproductions of both contemporary and ancient paintings.

These include works of Li Longmian whose horses were in demand during the Song Dynasty. Copies of the Yuan Dynasty's Ni Yun's painted bamboos are also for sale along with works copied from Ming and Qing Dynasty artists.

The Shanghai Friendship Store, the second largest in the People's Republic, next to Beijing's, also boasts a western-style supermarket on the ground floor where a huge variety of imported canned and packaged foods are displayed. Close by is the liquor and tobacco department where European wines, spirits and liquers as well as American, English and Japanese cigarettes are sold. There is a small, cafeteria-style restaurant on the second floor. Escalators, as well as elevators connect all four levels of the store.

Shanghai Art Gallery

Located at 226 Huangpi Bei Road, the Shanghai Art Gallery will interest visitors who wish to see examples of contemporary art from the region, photographs and woodblock prints.

Regular exhibitions will also reveal foreign masterpieces and more traditional works representative of Chinese styles.

TEMPLES AND GARDENS –
Tradition and Tranquility

Shanghai does not have as many temples as other major Chinese cities. This is because when the glorious religious traditions were being carved out in China's history, the city was a relatively minor fishing and trading settlement.

But there are a few temples to visit and the hottest favorite is the **Temple of Jade Buddha.** You will find it at 170 Anyuan Road in an industrial section in the north-west of Shanghai.

The visitor can take a number 16 bus from Yuyuan Bazaar which is at the north-eastern end of the old Chinese city. This is in the area of Fuzhou Road which you will have discovered when detouring off Nanjing Road.

The ride, if you manage to fight your way on board a bus, takes in about half of Shanghai. But, if you want to take a taxi from The Bund, it is a drive down Beijing Road, turning right into Jiangning Road. The temple is not very far from the Wusong River.

Dedicated walkers might like to set out along the roadway bordering Suzhou Creek with its busy water traffic providing interest, along with bridges, warehouses and a former Christian church that is now a municipal electricity research centre. The city fathers saw the light!

The Jade Buddha Temple is an active place of Buddhist worship and is named from two milky white Buddhas, each of which was carved from a single piece of Burmese jade. One Buddha reclines while the other sits on a lotus flower. They were transported to China from Burma in 1882 and are still objects greatly revered by the Shanghaiese, literally thousands of whom visit the temple daily.

The jewel-covered sitting Buddha on the lotus flower is depicted in his enlightenment. It is estimated the statue weighs about 1000 kilograms. Being transported into Nirvana, the second Buddha is more likely to represent an effigy under the influence of opium.

Both Buddhas were installed inside the brilliant, yellow-walled temple several years after it was completed in 1918.

About 7000 statues of Buddha, his disciples and heavenly effigies, including three gold-plated Buddhas in the main hall of the temple, are housed in the building and there is other statuary.

There are more than a score of resident Buddhist monks practising in the temple but they have done so only since 1980, after the nation's recovery from the Cultural Revolution during which period religious observance was banned and the temple was used for other purposes.

The temple just escaped being destroyed by Mao's Red Guards when the abbot secured the doors and stuck pictures of the Chairman all over them in a gesture of loyalty.

Maintained by small State stipends and donations, the monks operate a restaurant which vegetarians will find memorable. Their gift shop features tiny replicas of sandlewood gongs and drums.

Known as **Yufosi** by the Chinese, the Jade Buddha Temple should be avoided on February's Luna New Year – unless you want to compete with more than 20,000 Chinese Buddhists to meet the Buddhas.

Yu Garden

While you will not be permitted to take pictures, your photographic memory will recall interesting ceremonies conducted at dawn daily and around 4 p.m.

Longhua Temple and Pagoda

From downtown, take buses numbered 87, 41 or 44 to reach Shanghai's biggest and most venerable temple in the city's southern suburbs. The octagonal pagoda, seven storeys high of brick and wood, was originally constructed in 274 AD. The pagoda, which has been rebuilt a few times since the 10th century, has a bell hanging from each of its upturned eaves. Mao's guards used it as a propaganda pole but, because of the interest of tourists, it was renovated

out of its miserable condition of disrepair after China opened its doors to the west.

Part of a temple complex, largely of concrete updating from the Qing Dynasty, the Longhua Temple has five halls with courtyards, a bell tower and a drum tower. Once its peach blossoms were renowned throughout China and the world that was aware. But don't expect to find them in this place where the Kuomingtan were garrisoned before the second world war and where many Communist pioneers met their deaths.

The spring blossoms of the peach tree can be seen only in an area cordoned off and now known as Longhua Park.

Go further south-west to find 100 native species and almost 1000 miniature plants at the Shanghai **Botanical Gardens.**

The Bubbling Well Temple

Nanjing Xilu, the second section of Nanjing Road down from The Bund. once was known as Bubbling Well Road until the offending well was covered over.

Located opposite Jing' an Park near Nanjing Road, the temple of the same name is less interesting than its history. It was once under the domination of the abbott of Bubbling Well Road. Not only did this massive religious with shaved head have an incredibly rich wife. He had seven concubines and a private White Russian bodyguard as well!

More Temples and Pagodas

If the above are not enough to satisfy your need to seek out the temples of Shanghai, try the **Jiading Confucian Temple** built during the Song Dynasty in 1219 AD in the north-west of Shanghai. Though still a huge structure, it is today only about three-quarters as large as it was originally. The temple is now in ruins and is about 20 kilometres north of Hongkou Park near the Yangtze River but there is an interesting Chinese classical garden.

In the south-west is the 11th century **Songjiang Country Square Pagoda** and **Dragon Wall** which is near its original state. This pagoda can be climbed and has interesting Buddhist paintings and a Ming Dynasty glazed wall tile.

Italy's Pisa does not have a mortgage on leaning towers. China's, the **Huzhou Pagoda** circa 1079 AD, started tipping sideways two centuries ago. Almost 19 metres high, the Pagoda is now tipping from the vertical at an angle nearly two degrees more than the famous Leaning Tower of Pisa. But to see this relatively unknown wonder of the world, you will have travel to Sunjiang County, about 20 kilometres south-west of Shanghai, an area significantly older than the present day city.

Erected in the Song Dynasty, the **Cheng Huang Miao Temple of Town Gods** has had a varied history since it was built in the Ming Dynasty Yu Gardens to ensure the Shanghai area would remain at peace.

Yu Gardens

Locate yourself at the corner of The Bund and Nanjing Road, then walk south along the edge of the Huangpu River until the street name becomes Zhongshan Road. At about this time you will see Fuyu Road on your right and it is here that you will find the fully restored 16th century classical Chinese garden created for the Ming Manderin, Pan Yunduan for his father and family who were rich officials. Eighteen years in establishment, the garden occupies an area of about two hectares in Shanghai's old city area. But the Yu Garden seems much larger when one is strolling it. The garden came under fire during 1842's Opium War and later, during the Taiping Rebellion, because of its being home base of the small **Small Sword's Society,** it was destroyed by French troops.

The Society had supported the Taiping rebels and attacked the nearby French Concession.

Again badly damaged during the Boxer Rebellion, the garden has a museum which traces the Taiping Rebellion.

Today's visitor will find attractive Ming pavilions, covered walkways, rock gardens, lotus ponds, bamboo, shrubs and trees, all to be admired from winding paths and tiny bridges.

Animals, flowers and legends are depicted on traditional Suzhou bricks. The Yu Garden is closed at lunch time.

Hongkou Park

Within walking distance north of The Bund, Hongkou Park is also known as Lu Xun Memorial Park (146 Dong Jiangwan Road.)

The park's significance for the Chinese is that it is the setting for the **tomb of Lu Xun** who was a novelist regarded as being the father of modern Chinese literature. Despite the fact that he did not join the Communist Party, his works were revered by the youth and banned

Guyi Garden

by the Kuomintang from whom he sheltered in the French quarter. There is a museum in the park to his memory also. He died in 1936.

Xijiao Park and Shanghai Zoo

The zoo and this park are in Shanghai's western suburbs near Hongqiao Airport, If you happen to be staying at the Cypress Hotel which opened in 1982, you will find that you are quite close to Xijiao Park. It includes an open air theatre, a skating rink, some small pavilions and lakes. There is also a children's playground. With the Shanghai Zoo, the park is located at 2381 Hongqiao Road.

The zoo has about 500 species.

The Cypress Hotel, 2419 Hongqiao Road, much favored by foreign group tour operators, was China's first modern, western-style accommodation and restaurant complex designed by Shanghai's Industrial Design Institute. It features Szechuan and western cuisine. There is also an arcade of shops. It is set on grounds which were once Shanghai's golf club in the days of British occupation.

The park and zoo are also close to the Nikko Longbai Hotel (2451 Hongqiao Road), which is a joint Chinese-Japanese development. It

was completed in 1987 and is a lovely facility, particularly for business people. The hotel is very well managed by Japan Airlines' Nikko Hotels group.

Xijiao Park is also accessible to guests of more standard hotels in this open industrial zone near the airport. The hotels include the Chengqiao at 2226 Hongqiao Road, the New Garden Hotel at 1900, the Xijiao Dongyuan Guest House at 1591, and the Xijiao Guest House at 1921.

Guyi Yuan Gardens

This Ming Dynasty Garden of about six hectares is some 25 kilometres from the centre of Shanghai in Nanxiang Town, but is worth the trip because it contains several important relics including the **Stone Boat, Fuyun Pavilion,** the **Tang Dynasty stone pillars** inscribed with Buddhist scripture, and a **Song Dynasty stone pagoda.**

Other parks closer to the hub include **Zhongshan Park** which once housed the American St John's University on Changning Road and **Fuxing Park** on Chonqing Road.

Relics of Revolution and Religion

Sun Yat Sen's Shanghai Home

It is sometimes believed that Dr Sun Yat Sen lived all over China, such is the proliferation of former residences and memorials to the founder of the Chinese republic following the demise of the Qing Dynasty. But between 1918 and 1924, he lived at 7 Xiangshan Road, which was formerly in the French Concession, a short distance from Fuxing Park.

He lived here with his wife, Soong Qingling. Although he died in Beijing in 1925, she remained in Shanghai until 1937 under the observance of the Kuomintang and French police. She decided that her late husband's memorabilia should be displayed in the Shanghai residence which stands well back from the road and contains original objects as China's first president used them.

Soong Qingling's Former Residence

Sun Yat Sen's widow, who was also Honorary President of the People's Republic of China, spent much of her life at 1843 Huaihai Zhong Road. This 1920's-style house is set in a large garden and much of the furnishings have been kept exactly as they were in her lifetime. These include belongings located in her bedroom, upstairs office and the bedroom of the maid who was with her for a lifetime – Li Yan'e. One needs special permission to visit this house.

Soong Qingling's Tomb

Revered in China for her activities in international friendship in her declining years, Soong Qingling died in 1981. Her tomb can be found at the Wang Guo International Cemetery on Honqiao Road, not far from the Airport.

First National Congress of the CCP Site

In July, 1921, a secret meeting was held by the Chinese Communist Party at 76 Xingye Road – its first congress. The meeting place was subsequently seriously damaged, but was completely restored following the liberation of the city in 1949.

The room in which Mao Tse Dong met with 11 other delegates contains a table set with tea bowls and ash trays. The atmosphere is one of calm.

Two adjoining rooms display a pictorial history of the CCP. There are many photographs on the young Mao and other founders of the Party, the lives of all 12 delegates are traced and there is a copy of the first Chinese translation of Marx's Communist Manifesto.

The pictures are captioned in English. Do not go Mondays or Thursdays when this museum is closed.

Zhou Enlai's former residence

Visitors also need special permission to visit Zhou Enlai's home at 73 Sinan Road. He lived there in 1946 and operated the Communist

Party's Shanghai office from this residence which is now set up as a museum to his memory.

Xujiahui Cathedral

Shanghai's largest Catholic church was built in 1906 in the region which abutts the west end of the former French quarter. It was constructed in Romanesque style for the Jesuits who were the first Christian order to settle in the city in 1848.

The church is also known as **St Ignatius Cathedral** and is to be found at 158 Caoxi Bei Road in the Xujiahui District. It was used as the headquarters of rebel Taipings in the mid-1800s. It then became a large missionary centre with a seminary, college, school, orphanage, library and printing works. Its observatory still functions.

The cathedral has two bell towers of 50 metres height. These towers and the spires of the cathedral were badly damaged by Red Guards during the Cultural Revolution, but now they they have been completely restored.

With room for 2500 people for Mass on Sundays and other holy days of Catholic observance, the church has 19 altars.

Sun Yat Sen Mausoleum

Strolling through the old quarters

Nanshi – Old Town

A walk around Shanghai's former Chinatown, as opposed to the exclusive, foreign concession areas, should be planned in conjunction with a visit to the Yu Gardens. The old Chinese city is west of Renmin Road along Zhonghua Road. It is the oldest inhabited part of Shanghai. Here the missionaries first established their churches and communities although these churches no longer exist.

Originally, this relatively small area was walled and surrounded by a moat, but these protective fortifications were destroyed in the first years of this century. Once a maze of narrow streets and twisting alleys lined with hovels reeking of poverty, Nanshi was a place into which few Europeans were brave enough to venture.

The streets have been cleaned up yet the district still holds an atmosphere reflective of a former style of Chinese city life in its crowded lanes where there are still a few old buildings to see.

> **INFOTIP:** It is so easy to become lost in this rabbit warren that, again, you should carry in Chinese the address of your hotel or some central landmark from which you can orient yourself.

It is here that you may wish to sample a snack of the delicious dumplings for which Shanghai is famed. The most renowned of these dumpling stalls are at the gate of the **Yu Garden.**

At the north-east section of Nanshi is the **Yuyan Bazaar** where you will find traditional Chinese handicrafts such as bamboo and paper lanterns and intricately carved walking sticks, but try to avoid it on weekends when literally hundreds of thousands of locals and Chinese tourists from other parts of the PRC descend on the shops and stalls. There are also some interesting places to eat.

Take in the Temple Of The Town Gods (see Temples and Gardens section) which is a little further north again. Just behind it is the Garden Of The Purple Clouds Of Autumn, which, quite frankly, is not quite as colourful as its name, but worth a quick visit.

The French Quarter

You will find the colourful French quarter of Shanghai in the region around the famous Jinjiang Hotel which is at 59 Maoming Road, and Huaihai Road. To get there, it will take you about 45 minutes to walk from the Bund or, if you are game, take bus number 26 along Huaihai Road.

You will probably need sustenance after the walk or ride and the Jinjiang is probably a good place in which to have a meal, snack or drink. A former apartment complex in a tree-lined, residential avenue near **Fuzhou Park,** this hotel has four buildings and very nicely maintained gardens within its walls.

The Jinjiang has leadlight windows and parquetry floors and because of its facilities, including post and telecommunications office

Market Day

and conference centre, it is very popular with foreign business people.

You'll see these business people mixing with their Chinese counterparts and also students in the excellent ground floor bar which also offers live entertainment. Shops include a grocery outlet selling products imported from Hong Kong.

In the modern courtyard building, Premier Zhou En Lai and US President Richard Nixon negotiated the **Shanghai Communique** in 1972. While the South Wing is fairly basic, the elegant suites in the North Wing have been home to visiting foreign heads of State.

Both Western and Chinese food is good here and, although on the expensive side, the Jinjiang Nightclub is well worth a visit after dark.

The new deluxe, tower block next door opened in 1989.

The French quarter originally reached as far as The Bund, bordering the Old Chinese city. It was heavily populated by Chinese and also White Russians as well as Vietnam soldiers imported to protect the French. There are still some grand residential buildings in the quarter but good examples can be found in the area surrounding the Jinjiang Hotel. Go for a stroll around avenues lined by plane trees.

The atmosphere is still rather ethereal even though some of the parks are overgrown. Some were once cemeteries but any mausoleums are unlikely to be seen from the streets because of the denseness of the shrubbery.

Ultra-modern hotels in China can still be regarded as attractions in themselves, most having excellent varieties of cuisine, entertainments and public rooms which are worth inspecting. In the heart of the old, French quarter at 250 Huashan Road is the 40-storeyed Shanghai Hilton International which is about 15 minutes by taxi from The Bund and downtown.

This was the first major Hilton facility to be completed in China and opened in 1988. Guests can enjoy indoor swimming, tennis and squash. There are three executive storeys, eight restaurants and a business centre.

Children's Palace

If you are not a guest, call in to see the contemporary art works, and examples of ancient art. In the lobby is the **'story wall'** which comprises a four-storey-high mural of dozens of Chinese mythological characters. At this level, too, are bronze turtles and cranes cast in Thailand by an American who worked in a Thai bronze foundry. There is a dragon robe which was once possessed by a Chinese ambassador to Britain in the 19th century. It is displayed on the mezzanine floor. There are also works by Chinese, American and Japanese painters in the Teppan Grill and the Suiyuan Cantonese Restaurant features a beautiful lacquered plate in front of a blank screen. The delicate watercolours executed by **Zhu Qi Jian** when the Paris-trained, Shanghai artist was in his nineties, are also of interest.

Also located in the French quarter at 370 Hua Shan Road, a much older hotel, the **Jing An Guesthouse,** has a charming, private, lawn area and garden. It is favored by long-staying expatriate workers. Chinese-style rooms are huge and its restaurant is very well recommended.

Set near the top end of Nanjing Road, the Jing An was built as an apartment hotel for Germans living in Shanghai in the 1930s and reflects the ambience of that era. It was the first hotel in China to accept a credit card – Diners Club – and also has good communication services and shops.

You can gain a novel souvenir from a shop on the second level. Staff will photograph you against a backdrop of sharp-misted peaks or the Great Wall in garments similar to those worn by the Chinese in ancient times.

Completely of Chinese design, construction and management, the 23-level Shanghai Hotel at 460 Huashan Road is another French quarter accommodation and one of the city's newest. It opened in 1983. Designed for western comfort, it has deteriorated in maintainence somewhat, although it remains well filled with tour groups. There are some good shops, post office, telex, film developing, city tours and railway booking facilities.

PALACES AND PERFORMANCES

Children's Palaces

Soong Qingling, adopted the Russian concept of encouraging children between the ages of seven and 17 to develop various talents outside their normal school work. Instruction is given to youngsters in subjects such as painting, music, singing, traditional dances and opera, gymnastics, acrobatics, electronics, computing, craft work and model making.

The kids are taught in institutions known as Children's Palaces. Shanghai has 13 major ones including the first in that city which was established in 1949, soon after the People's Army marched in. This large institution, the Shanghai **Municipal Children's Palace** is at 64 Yan'an Xi Road which is not far from the Industrial Exhibition. It is regarded as one of China's best and located in an old mansion once owned by a wealthy Chinese family.

It is very much on the group tour itinerary trail, but individual visitors should ask at their hotel to arrange a time to go. Performanes are polished, energetic, friendly and skilled.

> **INFOTIP:** Ensure that your camera's flash is operating as performances take place indoors and it would be a pity to miss colourful shots of very appealing children.

Shanghai Concert Hall

The Shanghai Concert Hall is at 523 Yan'an Dong Road. But, as in the case of any of Shanghai's 30-odd theatres and halls and 70 movie theatres, it is wise to inquire at a China International Travel Service office and make a booking through its personnel rather than turn up, especially in the case of the **Acrobatic Theatre.**

Shanghai has an annual spring **Music Festival** so visitors dedicated to the performing arts should schedule their trip for May when thousands of professional and amateur singers, dancers and musicians take to the stage throughout the city.

The Shanghai Philharmonic Orchestra, the Shanghai National Orchestra, resident ballet, magic and acrobatics, puppet show, shadow boxing and song and dance troupes may have performances on during your visit.

You should also check if there are any visiting troups of ensembles from other parts of China.

The Shanghai Conservatory of Music

The Shanghai Conservatory of Music is in the French quarter at 20 Fenyang Rd , opened in 1927, was once a vital centre for European musicians but Western clasical music was frowned upon in the Cultural Revolution.

Avid followers of serious Western music will realise the number of talented young Chinese who have excelled in it and amazed western audiences since the form became re-recognised. Some have come out of this Conversatory.

Try to secure your tickets as early as possible before the seven o'clock Sunday performances which are usually sell-outs.

Visiting a local school

The Shanghai Art Theatre

At 57, Maoming Rd, the Shanghai Art Theatre in the French quarter too, is the former Lyceum Theatre which was very popular with the British in the 1930s.

The People's Opera Theatre

The People's Opera Theatre at 663 Jiujiang Road is the place where you can experience traditional Chinese opera.

This somewhat ponderous, high-pitched, but certainly very colourful musical form has limited appeal to some western visitors because they find it difficult to follow the plot. But a whole performance can be appreciated if it is explained to you by a local. It is not really expected that all foreigners will remain for the duration.

The Workers' Theatre is at 701 Fuzhou Road and it might be a novelty also to pop into a movie theatre for a sample of Chinese film making in which Shanghai is the nation's leading centre.

Factories and Friendship

It is basically only on an organised tour that the visitor will gain the opportunity to visit the factories which produce goods of interest to foreigners.

While these factories are set up to welcome tourists who may be offered tea or soft drinks and an explanation of their industries by individual managers, the problem is they are so hard to find. Unless located in the large factory sites on the outskirts of Shanghai (and these are most likely to be industries of little interest to the average visitor,) the small craft industries in the inner area of the city are most

likely to be located in basements or first floors of tenement buildings or hidden behind high walls.

Therefore, you are unlikely to just happen upon the factories which welcome tourists. However, if you see a sign in English outside a building marking a factory site, for example, Jade Factory, you can be fairly confident that you can just walk in off the street, inspect the process and that there will be a shop on the premises where you can buy, not necessarily at the prices of the Friendship Store and the big department stores along Nanjing Road.

So if you are in a hurry, book a tour which includes a factory visit. In Shanghai, you will certainly have a choice of jade, ivory and wood carving, embroidery, silk painting and dyeing, ceramics, carpet-making and calligraphy – to name but a few.

Working conditions are primitive by western standards but the industry (and eyesight) of the people is remarkable and at least one factory should be included on your Shanghai tour itinerary.

INFOTIP: Several western countries have banned the import of ivory in sympathy with the declining of the elephant population in Africa and India. Check customs before leaving your home country to avoid confiscation of ivory on your return. Camel bone looks very similar to ivory when the Chinese carving factories have finished with it. This particularly in jewellery, maybe a satisfactory substitute.

Through a China International Travel Service (CITS) tour it should also be possible to visit the apartment of one of Shanghai's working families. Essentially visitors will be taken to an apartment in which the family has its own private facilities. Tea is invariably offered and, through an interpreter, guests are free to question the tenant on family lifestyle.

Hitting the High Spots

Because Shanghai is such a vast metropolis, it is difficult to separate it into areas in which one is likely to find the place jumping after dark. However, there is quite a bit of action in the old French quarter near the Shanghai Hotel and Hilton Hotel.

At the Shanghai, along with the Park Hotel, on Nanjing Road, the discos are places to meet local girls, which can be a fun diversion.

But do not expect to recapture the infamous nights of Shanghai in the 1930s and 40s. While nightlife continues later in the big, joint-venture, international-style luxury hotels until about midnight, most Chinese have to be up very early. Even worse than Cinderella, the local talent tends to depart the scene by about 10 p.m. Nevertheless, Shanghai's nightlife is probably the most glittering in all of China.

As previously mentioned, the Jinjiang Hotel in the French quarter has a very lively disco. Alternatively its Club d' Elegance has a Japanese Karaoke Bar. There, customers can sing to pre-recorded music.

In the same district, at 849 Huashan Road, is the Dingxiang Garden. This is patronised by a fairly young crowd of Shanghaiese craving a bit of western culture but it is different from the discos operated by the modern hotels and is always interesting.

Around the Shanghai and the Hilton, a few enterprising entrepreneurs have opened up American-style bars. With neon signs illuminating them outside, they are not difficult to find and offer comfortable surrounds in which to enjoy a drink — at outrageous prices compared with similar establishments in most western cities. This is because the alcohol is often gained on the black market.

But, if you want to meet well-heeled locals and western expatriates, these are fun places which are often open until 2 a.m. or 3 a.m. Do not expect that your drink will be a quiet one. These bars are often quite noisy.

Closer to The Bund area, on the bank of the Huangpu River, you'll find the new, Shanghai Hyatt. Its bar has live entertainment. The Peace Hotel, just off The Bund on Nanjing Road, features a jazz band as previously mentioned. But the jazz tends to be more 1940's-style swing with numbers that the young Sinatra and Crosby made famous. More nostalgic than raging. And old time ballroom and Latin-American dancers will have a fine time between 8 p.m. and 11 p.m.

The Hua Ting Sheraton also provides night entertainment for guests. And possibly, they need it if they do not feel like going downtown because even though this is a top accommodation, best next to the Hilton in Shanghai, and very popular with business people and deluxe groups, it is located a long way from the city centre. At 1200 Cao Xi Bei Road, midway between the Airport and The Bund, it offers tennis, swimming, a health club and excellent business centre for those who wish to work or exercise as well as relax after dark.

The hotel does have one feature which could be a drawcard to non-guests as well, those hankering for Continental food and, perhaps, frustrated by the opening hours and crowds in the downtown restaurants. The Hua Ting operates Luigi's, which is Shanghai's only authentic Italian restaurant and the second in China. It is innovative cuisine presented by a chef from Italy's Abruzzo region and all apertifs, wines and liqueurs are Italian also.

Which brings us to an explanation for those who believe that their nights could be filled by an evening of dining.

Unless you plan to eat in one of the western-style hotels, your night of gourmandising will be cut short at around 8 p.m. Otherwise, you should make arrangements with management for a banquet or use of a special room reserved for foreign groups. The latter, of course, will cost more per head for the same food being served downstairs to the hordes but more staff must be retained for later diners.

Yet this is not meant to deter the visitor who really should experience each of the five major, great cuisines of China. Shanghai has got the lot. It is also fun and less expensive to eat with the crowd between 5 p.m. and 7 p.m.

There is a distinctive Shanghaiese cuisine, even though it is not one of China's major styles. Being so close to river and sea, seafood (particularly freshwater crab between October and December) and fish are specialities. Prawn dishes also figure prominently. Shanghai chefs tend to use a lot of oil, sugar, local wine, soy sauce and ginger in their creations, but the results are amazingly varied and appealing to all tastes — spicy to mild.

Being close to the Yangtze River, Shanghai naturally presents two cuisines based on the harvest that comes from it. The first is

Szechuan from that province, through which the mighty Yangtze flows. It is not for the faint-hearted and bland-palated as it is hot with peppers and garlic and can be sweet, salty or very sour and flavored with fennel or coriander, pepper and star anise.

Szechuan food is smoked, steamed or simmered and Szechuan Duck rivals the famed Peking Duck for tender taste and eating enjoyment.

The second major cuisine from a province bordering the Yangtze is **Hunan,** relatively unknown to westerners. Dishes are generally sweet, sour or spicy without the heat of Szechuan food. To experience the style, you could try sweet and sour fish, kidneys which are fried but oh, so tender, and delicate mushrooms are wonderful with chicken or fish. Try the Yueyanglou Restaurant, 28 Xizang Nan Road, tel. 285454.

Best known to westerners is the **Cantonese** style of cooking. It is the lightest of all styles, relying on rapid cooking, fresh produce and little fat. Steamed or stir-fried to retain the colours of crisp vegetables, it does not rely on heavy sauces because natural flavors are kept in such quick preparation. It also features tender roast meats and steamed fish, dumplings and patties.

Beijing cuisine reflects imperial tastes – crackling crispness outside with tenderness inside, no better reflected than in Peking Duck. It also reflects the days of Mongolian domination of the capital, hence **Mongolian hot pot** – lamb dipped in spicy sauces. Braising, steaming and deep frying or combinations of steaming followed by deep frying are methods of producing chicken and pork. With seafood, meats and vegetables also have high profiles in a richer style than Cantonese. Peking Duck which, when correctly served, comes with forcemeat dumplings and pancakes, is a banquet-style meal which should be ordered in advance and can take up to two hours (with other dishes) to enjoy. Depending on the restaurant, you can almost make an (early) night of eating entertainment with this.

If you order Peking Duck at the Park Hotel, you should be able to linger longer.

Roadside snacks

Fujianese is the fifth of China's major cuisines and is also unfamiliar to many westerners. The province has an extensive coastline so naturally seafood is prominent. Its soups are clear and delicate unless shark fin soup which is as thick as one of the hearty stews which also characterise the region. Fujian province is reputed to produce China's best soy sauce.

This cuisine can be experienced at the Minjiang, 679, Nanjing Road, tel: 241009 and the Overseas Chinese Hotel in the same street.

The major cuisines are supplemented by those of other provinces in China, notably **Yangzhou,** (closer to Cantonese style with pastries a specialty,) **Hangzhou,** (simpler than northern dishes with vegetarian emphasis including lotus stems and bean curd,) **Guangdong,** (very similar to Shanghaiese) **Suzhou** and **Wuxi,** also closely related.

Test Yangzhou at the Luyangoun or Yangzhou, respectively at 763 and 308 Nanjing Road, tel: 573221 and 222873. For Hangzhou, there's the Zhiweiguan Restaurant at 345, Fujian Zhong Road, tel: 224013, If you don't like Guangdong cuisine at the Mexican restaurant, 314, Shaanxi Nan Road, tel; 373991, you could switch to Cantonese which is served as well.

Experiment with either or both Suzhou and Wuxi at the well-known Renmin People's Restaurant, 226 Nanjing Road, tel: 537351.

You will also find food from other nations of South-East Asia in Shanghai. For Indonesian, there's the VIP Satay House, 849 Huashan Road, tel: 312211, and there is the Moslem Restaurant at 710 Fuzhou Road, tel. 224273.

There are numerous European quasi-French establishments in town but, quite frankly, Escoffier would turn in his grave! If you must have European, stick to the big hotels, otherwise hit the T.T. Fast Food Service, 74 Xixang Zhong Road, tel. 265853 for American-style junk food – which certainly will not take an evening to eat.

Schedule a 5 p.m. meal out of a hotel before going on to one of the entertainments listed under the section Palaces And Performances. And, even at 5 p.m., be prepared to battle for a seat at table, even to the extent of standing behind a customer who has almost finished a meal.

Shanghai Side Trips

Depending on your available time and money, Shanghai is the best travel hub in China from which to explore the beauty, culture and history of the PRC. But as this guide concentrates on the city itself, we confine suggestions for out-of-town diversions to relatively easily-reached attractions that can be experienced in three days at the most.

Suzhou – China's Garden City

Just 86 kilometres north and 75 minutes by rail away from Shanghai's central station is Suzhou which lies on the Grand Canal built in 605 AD. The canal linked Luoyang, which was then the capital of China, with the region south of the Yangtze River. This included Suzhou.

Suzhou's fame was established as a centre on a northern trade route on which its silks and foods were transported.

But basically, Suzhou's heritage is in its gardens.

In the 16th century, Suzhou had more than 100 gardens which had been created for generations of nobles, scholars and academics enchanted by the growth to come from its temperate climate. These gardens combined with many canals. Several have been closed but the character of the period remains in the city that was described by the first Europeans to visit it as The Venice Of The East.

Marco Polo, in the 13th century described Suzhou as 'a noble and great city.' Its 500-year-old tradition of silk making has been maintained with modern methods and the National Embroidery Institute contains China's best embroidery displays.

Suzhou was one of the few of China's most beautiful cities to escape the ravages of the Cultural Revolution.

Unless you are on an organised tour, you will have to catch one of numerous trains heading from Shanghai railway station on the Nanjing line. The main ticket office is at 230 Beijing Road, but unless you want to join queues to rival those at Ethiopian food handouts, forget it. Better to buy your ticket at the main Shanghai office of CITS at the Peace Hotel or China Travel Service, 104 Nanjing Road.

> **INFOTIP:** You'll be paying top Yuan for your tickets at what is called 'the tourist rate' and it is pretty hard to beat this system in Shanghai. Ticket prices for Chinese are much lower, but you would need to have made a local friend who will join the horrendous queues at the station ticket office to buy one on your behalf. Another alternative is to buy your ticket at a smaller station in one of the city's outer suburbs.

The trains for Suzhou leave from the main, or North Station on Tianmu Dong Road. As there is no Suzhou airport, your other travel alternative is a very cheap bus ride from Renmin Road's southern end.

It will not be hard for you to remember where you come into Suzhou by bus – the name of the road is the same as the one you left from in Shanghai. You will have just crossed the outer moat of this 3000-year-old city at Renmin Bridge. Just south of the Suzhou bus station you will find a taxi, pedicab or rickshaw prepared to take you along Renmin Road into the downtown area. Or else, next door to the taxi stand you'll find the ticket office and dock from which to take a Grand Canal boat ride to the cities of Wuxi or Hangzhou, respectively. More on this exciting option later.

If you have taken the train from Shanghai, you will arrive at the opposite end of this city of about 600,000 people. Either way you will get to the centre of things by central, Renmin Road.

To fully appreciate Suzhou, a day trip, from Shanghai and return is hardly sufficient and you will probably decide to spend one night there. There are several hotels. The Suzhou at 115 Shiquang Jie is a bit away from the centre. In the same compound is the Gusu Hotel, which is one of several curious semi-prefabricated motel-style accommodations that were manufactured in Australia and shipped to China soon after the Bamboo Curtain parted. It is a paradox to occupy a room where you may find pictures of Australian koala bears or that country's famous Ayers Rock decorating the wall.

Near Shiquang Jie Road the Nanlin Hotel is close to the dock and inter-city bus station. Downtown, you could try the Lexiang Hotel, 18, Dajing Xiang, which is off Renmin Road near the markets.

So, what is there to experience in Suzhou?

This is a walking city. Get a map from the CITS office (in the Suzhou Hotel enclosure) and start out along the inner city canals towards each destination.

Seven gardens are open to the public. These are not western displays of lawn and flowers, but intricate pavilions reflecting in water, outcrops af rock, pools and buildings play tricks with the eyes. In these gardens scholars used to contemplate; artists to paint.

The most interesting of the gardens is midway between the Nanlin and Suzhou and Gusu hotels, just off the juction of Shiquan Jie Road and Fenchuang Jie Road. You enter the **Wangshi** (or Master Of The Nets) **Garden** through a tiny alley west of the Suzhou Hotel and through a plain door that gives no indication of the loveliness that lies beyond. This 12th century garden was rehabilitated in the 1700s as an official's home and garden. There is a residential area, a main garden, and an inner courtyard garden in which is a cottage, formerly the study of the original Ming Dynasty owner. This is Suzhou's smallest garden but definitely a must if you have no time to see them all.

With five hectares of water – ponds and streams – crossed by bridges and dotted with islets of bamboo, the **Zhuozheng Garden** is the northern-most in the city, off Dongbei Jei Road. You will easily find it as the **Suzhou Museum** is in its grounds. Visit the museum to see silk samples from the Qing Dynasty, old maps of the city and the Grand Canal, and other relics excavated in the area. If you are walking around the city to discover all its gardens, this is the ideal place to start. The other major gardens of Suzhou are the **Shizilin Garden**, the **Dong and Quan Gardens** on opposite sides of a canal leading off the outer moat and the **Changlangting Garden** which is one of the oldest in the city, dating from the 11th century.

It is here that the visitor will find difficulty distinguishing the

Hangzhou West Lake

mirrored illusion in water from the reality of pavilions, a shrine, tower and other buildings. There are small streams which give the garden its alternative, **The Surging Wave Pavilion.** This garden is off Renmin Road up north of the Renmin Bridge in the city's south.

The Garden of Harmony or Yiyuan Garden is also a short distance from Renmin Road just west of the downtown area and is divided into east and west sectors.

Heading south from the railway station on Renmin Road you will see on your left **Bei Si** or the nine-storeyed, North Temple. One can climb the tallest pagoda located south of the Yangtze for a bird's eye view of the city and the farmlands beyond.

Silk factories are good to visit in Suzhou but the only way to get to them is on a CITS city tour. You will find embroidery, sandlewood fan and jade carving factories in the downtown area where also, around Guanqian Road, is the **Suzhou bazaar,** a rabbit warren of narrow streets. Here you will do your best shopping and find plenty to eat.

From the Suzhou bus station, take bus number 13 for a five kilometre ride south-east of the city for the 53-arched stone Tang Dynsty bridge which is one of the most impressive in China and crosses the Grand Canal. The bridge is called **Baodai Qiao,** or Precious Belt Bridge, after a Tang Dynasty official sold a valuable jewelled belt to finance the building of it.

However, the greatest pleasure of Suzhou is to wander its narrow

roads shaded with plane trees and watch the activity on the canals, particularly where there are bridges.

If you have opted to overnight in Suzhou, people-watching in the downtown area is a good nocturnal sport. You will find theatres and houses where stories are told and ballads sung. Occasionally the Suzhou Hotel has live entertainment.

Hangzhou, The China Of Dreams

While you can travel by bus from Suzhou to Hangzhou, the magically beautiful capital of Zhejiang Province, or travel direct by train

for three hours from Shanghai, the most novel way to reach the China of Dreams is by passenger boat along the Grand Canal from Suzhou.

If you are a romantic, and opt for the latter you can overnight on the 14 hour journey. But you will miss a lot in the early stages of the trip. Better to leave on the day boat, even though it departs from the dock by Renmin Bridge sometime before 6 am. The official departure time is 5.50 a.m., but like a lot of travel schedules in China, nothing is certain, except uncertainty. Even if you have already purchased a ticket through CITS in Suzhou, arrival at the dock no later than 5 a.m. is recommended. The second and evening departure from Suzhou is at 5.30 p.m. (or there abouts) and while a bunk costs only about twice

as much as the price of a seat on the daytime trip, you will see very little of Chinese life along the waterway before darkness falls.

INFOTIP: You will want to start eating your evening meal which is generally served within minutes of departure and it is a case of the quick or the dead as the shipboard cooks serve everything up at the same time. If you linger on the rail viewing life along the banks, you will probably go hungry, or, at the best dine on snacks from the bar where beer, spirits and soft drinks are available until about 10 p.m.

It is virtually impossible to appreciate Hangzhou in a one-day return trip from Shanghai but, no matter how you arrive, boat, train or bus, the logical way to return to your Shanghai base is by rail. The Hangzhou station fronts the lengthy Kai Hsuang Road, about halfway between Wangjiang Road to the south and Qintai Road to the north.

Buying a ticket back to Shanghai represents a luxury in Hangzhou because there is actually a separate ticket office for tourists. It is clearly signposted off the station's main concourse.

If you have arrived via the Grand Canal, the Hangzhou dock is just off Huancheng Bei Road, a few hundred metres east of its junction with Changzheng Road. The inter-city bus terminal is right on Changzheng, a short distance north of this junction,

All of these three arrival points are a hefty step from the central business and commercial area close to West Lake, but taxis are readily available.

West Lake: Above all, this is your reason to visit Hangzhou and the reason why the city has been China's premier tourist resort since the 17th century.

Hangzhou was the favorite watering hole of Qing emperors and anyone who was anybody in that era naturally aspired to visiting. Although not ancient by Chinese standards, Hangzhou began to develop when the Grand Canal reached it in 610AD. And, when the Southern Song Dynasty emperors chose it as their capital, it became briefly the largest and richest city in the world.

Marco Polo was awed by it.

West Lake is without doubt a most beautiful freshwater expanse surrounded on three sides by hazy, blue-green hills. There are several islands in the lake, the largest of which is linked to the city by a causeway. This island is called **Gu Shan** or Solitary Hill. It is the site of the Zhejiang Province Museum and Library.

The city itself is relatively new as most of old Hangzhou was destroyed during the Taiping Rebellion in early 1860s.

One of the best locations to stay in Hangzhou is the Central Overseas Chinese Hotel on Hubin Road, virtually fronting the lake. More expensive is the Hangzhou Shangri La Hotel on the north section of West Lake. You can reach both hotels from the railway station on a no 7 bus or, if you have arrived by boat or bus, seek out a no. 28 toi get you to the Shangri La.

Hangzhou is not the easiest of cities to experience on foot. The major attractions are scattered around the shores of West Lake, If you are not into hiring a bicycle from the several rental locations on Hubin

Road, close to the Overseas Chinese Hotel, a taxi from the rank in the small street at the side of the hotel is the best way to go. Best of all, if your time is limited, go straight to the Shangri La, even if you are not its guest and book a CITS city and lake tour from the office on the ground floor.

After West Lake, the major site of Hanghzou is the **Lingyin Si Temple** which dates from 326 AD although it has been wrecked, pillaged and then restored about 15 times since then. The temple today is basically a Qing Dynasty complex of buildings.

The temple complex is a fair way from the downtown area and you'd be best to take a taxi. The main structure is the Great Hall where a huge camphor-wood statue – a 30-year-old copy of a scuplture dating from the Tang Dynasty – guards an amazing collection of 150 small statues.

Another interesting temple building is the **Hall of the Heavenly Guardians.** Just as interesting as the temple itself is the hill in front of it where more than 300 sculptures, dating from the 10th century, have been carved into the rock. Behind the temple is lofty **Northern Peak,** a mini-mountain which, if you are very energetic, can be climbed and you will be rewarded by a quite magnificent view across West Lake.

Also a fair way from the centre is the **Pagoda of the Six Harmonies,** which is Hangzhou's best known. Located in the south-west of the city near the big bridge across the Qiantang River, it is more than 60 metres high. Again a taxi trip is recommended.

Quite close to the Shangri La Hotel, you will find the mausoleum of **General Yue Fei,** a 12th century Song Dynasty soldier whose skill, cunning and courage in the futile war against barbarian invaders was rewarded by palace intrigue ending in execution. The succeeding emperor, however, pardoned the corpse of this hardly-done-by patriot and interred the remains in the mausoleum. It contains a ceramic statue of the gentleman and paintings depicting his life and death.

The **Hangzhou Zoo** which can be reached from the Shangri La Hotel is quite interesting for its panda cage. If you cross the palm of a keeper with a suitable amount of renminmbi (FEC certificates are even more acceptable,) it is quite likely he will arouse one of the poor beasts and herd it to the front of the cage for your camera.

The zoo is in hilly country and covers a fair area. It is well signposted in English but unless you are fascinated by all the normal zoological fauna, make a trip to the pandas and then depart by either cab or bus back to your base at the Shangri La. Then, return to your own hotel if this is not it or spend your time profitably visiting **Gu Shan** or Solitary Hill island close to the lake boat embarkation point a few hundred metres from the Shangri La's main entrance.

There are several small, cheap restaurants on the island which specialise in dishes caught fresh from the lake and Hangzhou's most famous restaurant, the Louwailou, is located in a peaceful park setting.

The provincial museum on the island is, quite frankly, nothing to write home about. If you are pressed for time, forget it.

If you haven't yet bought silk, the Hangzhou Silk Printing and Dyeing Complex is the largest silk factory in China. Book with CITS for a visit.

Nightlife in Hangzhou. The downtown area abounds with bars around the Overseas Chinese Hotel but, if the night is fair, why not experience a moon and starlit stroll around the shores of West Lake or take a one hour boat ride from the landing stage opposite the Shangri La.

INFOTIP: With a population of only 1 million, Hangzhou is an uncrowded city compared with Shanghai from Monday to Saturday. But on Sunday, literally hundreds of thousands of day trippers from Shanghai and other nearby cities arrive. Try to schedule your visit accordingly.

Finally, if you have included Hangzhou in your advanced Shanghai planning, you can leave the People's Republic of China from the Hangzhou airport which has five scheduled flights a week to Hong Kong and daily flights to Guangzhou (Canton) and Beijing.

Along The Mighty Yangtze

It would be a pity for anyone who has travelled to Shanghai not to have some experience of the mighty Yangtze River which is China's longest and the third longest river in the world – 6300 kilometres.

Regarded as being among the most spectacular river scenery on earth, the **Three Gorges,** a 189 kilometre stretch through Xiling, Wu and Qutang gorges – rugged shores and towering peaks – is a side trip which will take a minimum of five days from Shanghai and return.

It can be done by flying from Shanghai Airport to Chongqing via Wuhan. There you have two alternatives – to join a luxury vessel which will take you through the gorges with stop offs for day sight-seeing at fascinating towns and villages or to board an East Is Red ferry. These ferry boats – there are more than 40 of them with the same name along the Yangtze – are the transport of the people and conditions aboard are, to say the least, spartan.

You cannot just board one of the luxury cruise vessels but must book in advance, ideally through a travel agent in your home country, or from Hong Kong's Travel Asia Limited at 30-32 Aguilar Street, tel. (852) 5-265661/2. Your last booking resort is the CITS office in Shanghai but this might have to be on a cancellation basis as these popular vessels are booked out months in advance by foreign tour groups.

If you do book a luxury cruise, you will not only experience magnificent scenery, villages still relatively unspoiled by tourism and the cuisines of the provinces through which you pass. You will have a fabulous time on board ships with twin-bedded accommodation and private facilities, swimming pool, restaurant (all meals are included in the fare) bar and dance floor, plus medical, hairdressing, postal and banking facilities. Service aboard these ships compares favorably with the best of the new, luxury hotels in Shanghai. Guides and inter-preters are on board to explain the legends and teeming lifestyle of the Yangtze River people. An experience not to be missed if you can afford the time.

But, if time, money, or both are a problem, you can have an experience of the lower reaches of the Yangtze out of Shanghai, either as far as Wuhan, which will take a similar amount of time and,

most likely, on an East Is Red ferry, or you need travel only to the city of Nanjing.

If Nanjing is to be your destination, buy a one way ticket and return the 305 kilometres to Shanghai by train. It's about a four hour rail journey.

You can buy ferry boat tickets for Nanjing and Wuhan at 222 Renmin Road in Shanghai and the boats leave from Shilipu Wharf on The Bund, four major streets south of Nanjing Road.

The ferry to Nanjing will take almost 20 hours which will allow a one-day experience of Nanjing with a one-night stay in the city before training it back to Shanghai.

Nanjing – Capital Of Eight Dynasties

You will arrive by boat at the dock which is at the western end of Zhongshan Beilu, the road which leads into Zhongshan Road, the main drag of Nanjing. Orientate yourself on this thoroughfare at the Jingling Hotel which, with 36 storeys, is pretty hard to miss. It is in the centre of Nanjing and one of China's largest high-rise buildings. It is probably the best place to stay. The hotel has a revolving restaurant, pool and sauna.

But middle rung accommodation can be found at the Nanjing Hotel less than halfway between the ferry wharf and the Jingling on Zhongshan Beilu and accessible by the number 16 bus from your river arrival point or by trolley bus number 32 if you have arrived in the city by train. There are several other hotels with western-standard tourist accommodation, but few in the budget class.

The word Nanjing means southern capital and indeed, through its 2000-year history, eight different dynasties have proclaimed it as such. Nanjing was, in the 19th century, the rebel Taiping Heavenly Kingdom's headquarters but was devastated after the Qing Dynasty's army backed by foreign troops broke the revolt with bloody massacres and wholesale destruction in the city.

The city was the Ming Dynasty's capital and although its ancient walls are now broken, they are still massive ruins. The wall was the world's longest city fortification ever built and you can see a section of its 20 or more kilometres remaining by walking west from Zhongshan towards the Yangtze River along Beijing Xilu.

If you walk south from the wall along a canal until you reach Shengzhou Road, then turn right again at Zhongshan Nanlu, you will find the Zhonghua Gate which is one of the 13 city gates from the Ming period still standing. Vaults in the four rows of gates are now devoted to tourism – eateries and souvenir shops. North the gate is the **Taiping Museum** which is in a former private mansion and adjacent to **Zhan Yuan Garden,** which was enjoyed by the Ming Dynasty's first emperor. The museum includes duplicates of written material, relics and maps chronicling the rebellion.

Now, proceed north along Taiping Nanlu until you reach Zhongshan Donglu. Turn right. To your left are the buses which leave for Qixia Mountain which has three magnificent peaks. This is a wonderful scenic spot particularly in autumn when maple-covered slopes are ablaze with color. Beneath the middle peak is the **Flying Phoenix,** a 1500-year-old monastery with a buddha carved from a single block of white marble.

Nanjing

Vegetarian Monastry

If you opt not to go to Qixia, on your right you will see the ruins of **Hong Wu's Ming palace,** Hong Wu being the founding emperor of the Ming Dynasty. Diagonally opposite, to the left is the **Nanjing Museum.** This has an interesting collection of relics from neolithic to modern times. The major building resembles an ancient temple.

The so-called Purple Mountains ring Nanjing and, continuing east from Hong Wu's burial place, you will find one of Nanjing's major attractions – the **Mausoleum of Dr Sun Yat Sen,** founder of the Republic of China and still revered by the people of the PRC as the huge tomb and its marble entrance indicate.

The mausoleum is part of the **Linggu Park** which also includes an American-designed nine-level pagoda built in the 1930s to revere Kuomintang casualties in the 1926-28 revolution.

The tomb of **Hong Wu** is also in the park on Zijin Mountain's south slope but because of the destruction during the Taiping Rebellion only the tomb guardians, courtyard and stone gate remain.

The park has many other attractions – avenues of stone figures and animals, the **Linggu Temple** and **Pine Wind Pavilion.** Also, the Beamless Hall is part of the brick temple built by Hong Wu while constructing his final resting place.

Back along familiar Zhongshan Lu you will find, diagonally opposite

at a roundabout, the **Drum Tower** and the **Bell Tower.** The road becomes Daqing Lu and, on the way to the railway station is central **Xuanwu Lake Park** with islands, bridges, the Nanjing Zoo and a theatre.

If you have not arrived along the Yangtze – or perhaps do not even intend leaving by it, check out the Yangtze River Bridge, just north of the dock, before you leave Nanjing. It is hailed in China as a triumph of revolutionary perseverance and engineering skill. The bottom of the swirling Yangtze River is mud for about 30 metres down and the soft bottom defied even Soviet Union engineers who originally were contracted to built the bridge. They failed, but the Chinese kept going and succeeded with a pylon system which has become a benchmark for bridge builders throughout the world faced with similar problems.

Nightlife, again, is not in the restaurants which tend to close at 8 p.m. But do eat,particularly in dear old Zhongshan Lu or Nanlu. Nanjing has imperial traditions in its cuisine and it is said that Peking Duck was invented here.

There is live entertainment at night in the Jinling Hotel's revolving restaurant, the first of its kind in China, with a terrific view day or night, and a less expensive piano bar at ground level.

Otherwise, go for a walk by the river.

MUSEUMS

Shanghai Art and History Museum

There are 106,000 precious cultural exhibits housed in the Shanghai Art and History Museum located at 16 Henan Nan Lu which is two major blocks from Nanjing Road and one from The Bund. You can visit it after browsing the book shops in Fuzhou Road which bisects Henan Road.

The museum was founded late in 1952 to collect, preserve, study and display relics of China's past dynasties. It also publishes picture albums and books on its collections.

These collections are located on three levels and represent the finest in China. On the first floor is the Chinese bronzes exhibition generally from Shang (1600 – 1027 BC) and Western Zhou (1027 – 771 BC.) dynasties. Reflecting China's slave society and early stages of feudalism, the shape and pattern of the bronzes have embodied a unique artistic style and outstanding casting techniques.

Exhibits include instruments of torture, weapons, tools, mirrors, food and wine containers and impressive cauldrons.

The ceramics exhibition occupies the second floor and includes a diverse collection from roughly baked pottery pieces 7000 years old unearthed in the Yellow River and Yangtze River basins. Also, there are fine porcelains of more recent eras. There are examples of pottery from the neolithic period, so-called black pottery, primitive works from the Shang Dynasty and clay figures of warriors and horses of the Qin Dynasty.

Two warriors are the first of about 10,000 life-size figures from the huge tomb dug out at Xian in 1974. The excavation was of the tomb of Emperor Qin Shi and the finds substantiated that until this period, slaves and statues of households were buried along with their lord.

Glazed pottery from the Tang Dynasty (618 – 907 AD) and excellent ceramics from Song, Yuan, Ming and Qing Dynasties are displayed.

The development of ceramics reflected the social relations and ideologies of varying periods in China's chequered history. After the Tang Dynasty, chinaware was introduced to the world beyond the empire. Then China became known as the Land of Porcelain.

While the third floor is dominated by a collection of Chinese paintings, there are also displays of impliments used for painting and calligraphy and a very good exhibition of Buddhist stone sculptures.

The paintings are rich and colourful in themes and styles. Here they are grouped under seven categories. The first three introduce the early development of Chinese painting in displays of precious remnants of the first schools and styles. These include the colour designs on neolithic pottery, painted wooden carvings which were unearthed at the tombs of the Shang Dynasty rulers and paintings on silk. The latter come from the Warring States period (480 -221 BC) and the Han Dynasty (206 – 25 BC.) These silk paintings were found in an ancient tomb in Changsha.

The other four categories comprise paintings on various themes and in the different styles of the Tang, Song, Yuan, Ming and Qing Dynasties. They are characterised by fine, colourful brushwork, both detailed and free. They include vivid expression and bold outline with use of Chinese ink. The collections of traditional Chinese realistic paintings and wash paintings depict mountains, rivers, figures, birds and flowers. Many visitors acclaim them as the epitome of perfection.

The museum frequently has short term exhibitions of specific cultural relics. On the third floor is a shop selling postcards and reproductions. There is also a small cafe where tea, soft drinks and snacks are on offer.

> **INFOTIP:** The toilets in the museum are very cleanly maintained, but as even a cursory examination of the collections is a minimum half day affair, take some toilet paper with you from your hotel as, chances are, you will not find any in the museum's facilities!

Museum of Natural History

A few blocks away from The Bund on the intersection of Henan Road and Yan'an Dong Road, you will find the Shanghai Museum of Natural History. It is at number 260 Yan'an Dong. The museum opened in 1963. It features different exhibitions on a regular basis and permanent displays cover both ancient and modern times.

Perhaps its most fascinating exhibit is a dinosaur from Szechuan Province believed to be 140 million years old, but on the ground floor there is also an amazing display of preserved human bodies more than 3200 years old.

The museum is closed on Tuesdays and Saturday mornings. Explanatory films are also shown on a regular schedule during opening hours — 8.30 a.m. to to 10.30 a.m. and 1 p.m. to 3.30 p.m.

PART III
Accommodation

HOTELS

General Notes

There are a number of high class hotels that are open to tourists and business visitors to Shanghai, which offer serene surroundings, spacious rooms, complete facilities and best services.

Some of these hotels are suitable for holding international conferences of different scales.

The tallest hotel in Shanghai, The Shanghai Guesthouse, is equipped with modern projecting and accoustic as well as simultaneous translation facilities.

Within a decade China has gone from a nil balance in the luxury hotel register to a resounding credit. The traveller will be pleasantly surprised at the service and the appointments of the major hotels. Tariffs are, by and large, competitive too, it is however advisable that bookings are made through major travel operators.

There is no official or Government controlled classification of public accommodation of public accommodation either national, or in Shanghai itself.

The Chinese Tourist bureau or travel operators, can provide you with full details of available accommodation and up-to-date tariffs for all hotels listed here.

We have simplified the information as far as possible by indicating facilities such as air-conditioning, television, refrigeration, telephone, restaurant, room service, swimming pool etc.

Legend

rm	rooms
AC	air-conditioning
Tel	rooms with telephone
TV	rooms with television
PB	rooms with private bathroom
R	restaurant
B	bar
C	coffee shop
S24	24-hour room service
P	babysitting
FE	foreign exchange
ReF	refrigeration in rooms
NC	night club
SP	swimming pool

INFOTIP: Most of the Hotel restaurants in China, offer Chinese and Western cuisine. Recreational grounds and business facilities are normally available. The aim of Hotels in China is 'Reputation First, Guest First'.

Shanghai Mansions

SHANGHAI

Cypress Hotel
2419 Hongqiao Road   **Tel.** 329388
The Cypress Hotel is located only a few kilometres from the airport. At the hotel it is also possible to stay in tiny 'apartments' which have lounge rooms and small kitchenettes.

rm-158 AC Tel TV PB R B C P FE

Da Hua Guest House
914 West Yan'an Road   **Tel.** 523079
Centrally located, the Da Hua Guest House has postal facilities and barber and souvenir shops

rm-89 AC Tel TV PB R B C FE

Donghu Guest House
167 Xin Le Road   **Tel.** 370050
The Donghu Guest House is situated in inner Shanghai and offers tennis courts and postal facilities.

rm-120 AC Tel TV PB R P FE

Park Hotel
170 Nanjing Road (West)
Tel. 225225
The Park Hotel is located in the city centre.

rm-170 AC Tel TV PB R B C FE NC.

Hengshan Guest House
534 Heng Shan Road   **Tel.** 377050
Located close to the city centre, the Hengshan Guest House has massage, taxi and postal services.

rm-202 AC Tel TV PB R B C FE

Peace Hotel
20 Nanjing Road (East)   **Tel.** 211244
The Peace Hotel has Chinese and Western restaurants and is located close to central Shanghai.

rm-342 AC Tel TV PB R C FE NC

Cypress Hotel

Hongqiao Guest House
1591 Hong Qiao Road **Tel.** 372170
The Hongqiao Guest House is located close to the airport.

rm-25 AC Tel TV PB R P FE

Overseas Chinese Hotel
104 West Nanjing Road
Tel. 226226
The Overseas Chinese Hotel is centrally located and has postal facilities and a barber shop.

rm-115 AC Tel TV PB R C FE

Jing'An Guest House
370 Hua Shan Road **Tel.** 563050
This guest house is situated close to the city and has Chinese and Western restaurants.

rm-111 AC Tel TV PB R B C FE

Jinjiang Hotel
59 Maoming Road (South)
Tel. 582582
The Jinjiang Hotel is located in central Shanghai and features a shopping arcade, tennis courts and postal and taxi services.

rm-622 AC Tel TV PB R B C P FE

Rui Jin Guest House
118 Rui Jin Er Road **Tel.** 372653
This guest house is located in the city centre and has postal facilities and Chinese and Western restaurants.

rm-55 AC Tel TV PB R FE

Shanghai Hotel
505 Wulumuqi Bei Lu **Tel.** 312312
This hotel is conveniently located in central Shanghai.

rm-604 AC Tel TV PB R B C FE

Haihong Hotel
528 Shui, Dian Road   **Tel.** 662392
Haihong hotel is located 3 miles
(7 km) from Shanghai Railway and
near the central Shanghai and has a
hairdresser, post office, typewriting,
telex etc.

rm255 TV Ref PB Tel B C

Qin Nian Hui Hotel
123 Xi Zang Road   **Tel.** 261040
Located on the centre of the city
with a shop and disco bar.

rm168 TV AC Tel Ref R NC

Tian Ma Hotel
471 Wu Zhong Road   **Tel.** 328100
Located at the Hongqiao Diplomatic
area and the international centre,
one will find himself in an exotic and
artistic atmosphere

rm200 TV AC Ref NC FE S24 B R PB
SP

Hilton Hotel
250 Huanshan Road   **Tel.** 550000

AC TV P S24 R Ref NC

Shanghai Mansions
20 North Suzhou Road   **Tel.** 246260
The Shanghai Mansions are situated
only two kilometres from the railway
station and have postal facilities.

rm-249 AC Tel TV PB R B C FE

Xi Jiao Guest House
1921 Hong Qiao Road   **Tel.** 379643
The Xi Jiao Guest House has
attractive indoor and outdoor
gardens as well as a dance hall and
tea house. It is located in suburban
Shanghai.

rm-86 AC Tel TV PB R B P FE

Xingguo Guest House
72 Xing Guo Road   **Tel.** 374503
The Xingguo Guest House is located
close to central Shanghai and has
barber and souvenir shops.

rm-53 AC Tel TV PB R P FE

Chengqiao Hotel
2266 Hongqiao Road   **Tel.** 329220
The hotel is located to the western
sector of the city en route to Hongqiao International Airport. There is a
beauty parlour postal and telecommunication services.

rm130 AC R Tel TV PB B C FE

Park Hotel

Shanghai Hotel

HANGZHOU

Only standard facilities are available for the following hotels.

Dragon Hotel
Shuguang Road **Tel.** 54488

Friendship Hotel
53 Pinghai Road **Tel.** 22951

Hangzhou Hotel
78 Beishan street **Tel.** 23701

Overseas Chinese Hotel
15 Hulin Lu **Tel.** 23401

Shangri-La Hotel
78 Beisham Road **Tel.** 22921

Xinqiao Hotel
176 Jiefang Lu **Tel.** 23701

SUZHOU

Nanyuan Guest House
249 Shi Quan Street **Tel.** 27661
Located in the centre of Suzhou, facilities include clinic, post and telecommunication services, barber shop and beauty parlour.

rm116 AC TV Tel R FE S24

Xucheng Hotel
120 Sanxiang Road
Tel. 34855 or 31928
Located in the attractive district where the ancient city and the new town are connected.

AC R B TV

149

PART IV
Practical Information

PRACTICAL INFORMATION

Advance Planning

When to Visit

The best seasons in which to visit Shanghai are Autumn and Spring when the average maximum temperature is around 24°C (75°F).

Spring gardens, blossoming trees and russet yellow and gold leaves being shed in Autumn are spectacular in this beautiful season.

Shanghai is fairly humid all year round because of its high rainfall but the humidity becomes even worse in Summer when Shanghai is a place to be avoided.

Semi tropical conditions prevail then in Shanghai and the Yangtze valley. The Chinese nickname for Nanjing, Wuhan and Chonquing during Summer is the three furnaces and conditions can be extremely unpleasant.

What to bring

Documents: passport, credit cards. You will be issued with Foreign Exchange Certificates on arrival in China.

Americans: US Customs will require records of overseas purchases.

Clothing: Unless you have a business meeting or a formal function planned in Shanghai bring only comfortable casual clothes.

We hope that you will not work too hard while you are there – there are far better things to see and do.

For a night out we can only think of only a couple of clubs and scarcely a restaurant where you might regret their absence.

Ladies of course have no such problem, but remember when you are packing to avoid bringing any revealing clothing which will attract some disapproval and a lot of attention.

Whatever season you visit Shanghai in you will need sturdy comfortable shoes or boots or you will be sorry to miss the lovely outdoor walks.

Don't forget your camera, there are few places you can't miss it more.

> **INFOTIP:** If you plan to be travelling about China and Shanghai is just one stopping point you may be travelling through several different weather zones (except in summer when it is hot everywhere). Try and pack clothes which you can wear in layers which can be taken off or added to as the weather allows as the Chinese are fairly strict about baggage allowances (20 kg).

Odds and Ends: Some western goods are available from Friendship Stores in Shanghai but to be on the safe side it is probably best to bring your own sunscreen, shampoo, laundry powder, batteries, camera film, tooth paste and contact lens solutions.

Many brands of western cigarettes are available in China at reasonable prices but if you are very particular it may be a good idea to bring your own cigarettes with you.

Coffee again is something which is available in China, but not always exactly when you want it. If you like regular cups of coffee throughout the day you should bring your own instant coffee, sugar and longlife or powdered milk with you.

If Chinese tea is not to your taste it is also a good idea to bring your own tea with you to China.

Medical Tips: Travel insurance is a good idea when you are travelling to China as the costs of hospitalisation are high.

Bring your own medicines for throat, stomach and headaches with you to China as these types of medicines are often unavailable.

If you are taking any kind of medication make sure that you bring enough with you to last throughout your stay in China.

People with hearing aids should bring an adequate supply of batteries with them.

If you plan on travelling to rural areas of China in Spring or Summer a course of anti-malaria tablets is recommended.

Immunisation certificates are required by tourists who have passed through areas infected with yellow fever in the six days prior to their arrival in China.

Before you leave for China it is recommended that you visit your doctor for current information on immunisations.

Entry Regulations

To travel to China you must have a visa and passport which will be valid for the duration of your stay in China. To obtain a visa, contact the Chinese Consulate in your own country or a branch of the China International Travel Service (CITS – see Tourist Services). If you are travelling to China as part of a tour group your travel agent will organise a visa for all the group members to travel on.

Customs

When entering China you will be asked to fill in a customs declaration form on which you list all items such as cameras, electronic goods, watches or jewellery which you are bringing into China with you. Remember to declare any gifts which you bring with you. You must keep the carbon copy of your declaration form with you until you leave China as customs officials may ask you to prove that you are in fact taking all items listed on the form with you from China.

You are permitted to bring up to 400 cigarettes, 2 bottles of alcoholic beverages not exceeding 3/4 and up to 6 dozen rolls of camera film with you to China.

You are not permitted to bring explosives, firearms, Chinese currency, pornographic material, addictive drugs or radio transmitting equipment with you to China.

> **INFOTIP:** Keep all your exchange receipts from changing foreign currency to Chinese with you as you may have to produce these before any excess currency certificates you have will be changed back to foreign currency when you leave China.

Currency

You may not bring Chinese currency with you into China, though bringing in foreign currency is permitted. There is no limit to the amount of foreign currency you can bring into China.

When leaving China you may take with you Foreign Exchange Certificates (tourist money) but not Renminbi (RMB).

Getting to Shanghai

By air: Many major airlines offer flights to Shanghai. There are direct flights between Shanghai and the major cities of Europe, Asia, the United States and Australia. There are also regular flights between Hongkong and Shanghai and a variety of domestic flights from within China.

By rail: Train services to Shanghai from all over China are regular and efficient. Bearing in mind that train travel is time consuming it is also a wonderful way to see more of China. Travelling 'soft class' on Chinese trains is quite comfortable and express services and sleepers are available.

By sea: Some cruise lines do stop at Shanghai and you should consult your travel agent if you wish to reach Shanghai by sea. There is also a ferry service between Shanghai and Kobe in Japan run by the China Ocean Shipping Agency and the same company runs passenger ships between Hongkong and Shanghai.

Electricity

Voltage differs in each area of China so try not to bring too many electrical appliances with you – and bring adaptor plugs for any appliances you do bring.

Voltage is usually 220-240 V and plugs usually have two either round or flat pins.

Entertainment

Children's Entertainment

There are a few parks in Shanghai but children should be kept amused by any sightseeing that you do. They will especially enjoy the acrobatic and puppet shows which are given around Shanghai.

Babysitting

Tourists do not usually bring their children with them to China, so most hotels will not have babysitting facilities. If a babysitter is required you can always try asking hotel staff to see if something can be arranged.

Practical Information

Dance

European and Chinese ballets are both performed in Shanghai. Both are of a high standard but for tourists the Chinese dance may be more interesting. The ballets are often based upon tales of ancient China.

Cultural shows

Featuring the songs and dances of China's various ethnic groups are also very entertaining. These shows are usually brief and move quickly from one national group to the next so there is no time to get bored. The costumes of the different groups are especially interesting.

Music

The works of European composers are popular in China and though concerts are not quite up to international standards they are highly entertaining.

Operas

Chinese operas are dramatic performances that tourists either love or loathe. They have all the ingredients necessary to move the plot along – wicked villains, bold heros and fair damsels – but props are kept down to a bare minimum and mime is used extensively and so people who do not speak Chinese are often left confused and bored by the whole experience. If you have a guide who can translate for you you will enjoy the opera much much more.

Even if you do not have a guide to explain things to you Chinese opera can still be enjoyed. The costumes are magnificent and performers wear elaborate masks, with spectacularly malevolent creations being donned by the actors who play the villains. Acrobats also appear in the opera and liven things up.

You may find that on a group tour your group will be edged out of the theatre shortly after the performance has begun. This is as your guide will probably expect that westerners will not enjoy the opera. If you ask your guide if you can arrange to see an entire opera they will probably be happy to oblige.

In Shanghai the style of opera known as yue ju is popular and these are the operas most enjoyed by tourists. In yue ju string instruments are used rather than percussion and so the music sounds 'normal' and not so outlandish.

Shadow Puppets

Shadow puppeteers have been enchanting audiences in China for over two thousand years.

The puppeteer moves flat puppets behind a white silk screen whilst a bright light causes a shadow to be cast on the screen in the shape of the puppet. The puppeteers also provide voices for their creations which can be made to sing or dance as the story requires.

Ancient legends are a popular basis for shadow puppet plays and you will find both professional and amateur groups giving performances. The plays might sound like something for children but adults enjoy them too so don't miss out on a chance to see a shadow puppet play.

Acrobats

Acrobatic performances featuring jugglers, comedians, trapeze artists, contortionists and magicians are often given for tourist groups and are really very enjoyable. Chinese acrobats train to a very high standard and, like the shadow puppets, their shows are for adults as well as children.

Paper Dragon Maker

Festivals and National Holidays

Spring Festival or Chinese New Year

The Spring Festival is a Three day holiday celebrating the new year. During this festival the Chinese like to buy new clothes, settle debts, exchange gifts and enjoy rich food.

The **Lantern Festival** marks the end of the Spring Festival in a noisy, colourful celebration.

> **INFOTIP:** The dates of these festivals are determined by the Chinese lunar calendar and so fall on different days each year. Ask your travel agent before you leave for China about current dates for Chinese festivals.

Qingming

The Qingming festival honours the dead and this is the traditional time for the Chinese to visit and tend to the graves of their ancestors.

Dragon Boat Festival

The Dragon Boat Festival commemorates the death of the ancient poet Qu Yuan who drowned in the Hunan province. The Dragon Boats in the festival symbolise the boats that raced to save Qu Yuan but were too late.

Rice cakes with nut and date centres are traditionally eaten during this festival.

Mid Autumn Festival

During this festival people look forward to a plentiful harvest and watch the full moon. Cakes made from dates, sesame and lotus seeds are eaten during the Mid Autumn Festival.

National Holidays

January 1	**New Years Day**
January or February	**Spring Festival (Chinese New Year)**
May 1	**Labour Day**
October 1	**National Day**

Getting Around in Shanghai

Public Transport

Public transport is certainly the cheapest way to get around Shanghai but it is not the easiest. Firstly all public transport guides and maps are only available in Chinese, so you could have trouble finding your way about and secondly buses are very very crowded so travelling on them is certainly not a pleasant experience.

Buses

Shanghai's bus routes can take you past some of the city's premier tourist attractions if you are confident enough to get on board.

The first problem for people who don't speak Chinese is paying the fare. Fares are calculated on distance so you must be able to name your destination in Chinese when you get on the bus. One way to get around this is to have someone at your hotel write down your destination in Chinese and you can show this to the driver. Make sure you have the name of your hotel also written down so you can find your way home.

The second problem is fighting your way on and off the buses which always seem to be crowded.

Taxi

Travelling by taxi is an inexpensive and convenient way to get around Shanghai. Taxis don't wait at stands or cruise the streets looking for customers in Shanghai but they can be easily arranged and most hotels, shops and restaurants will call a taxi for you.

Taxi drivers do not accept tips and will give change to the exact amount.

If you are planning some sightseeing in Shanghai and want to get from place to place easily then consider hiring a taxi for a day or for a few hours. It doesn't cost very much and it means that you won't have to waste time getting about.

Shanghai Tourist Taxi Company: Is a State-owned enterprise specialising in providing tour buses and cars. Located at 16 Wuzhong Road, tel 383420.

Cruising in Yangtze

Getting Out of Shanghai

By air: Flights leave Shanghai for a variety of international and domestic locations.

Major airlines with offices in Shanghai
CAAC Tel. 535953
CATHAY PACIFIC Tel. 377899
NORTHWEST AIRLINES Tel. 377387
SINGAPORE AIRLINES Tel. 328729
UNITED AIRLINES Tel. 530210

By rail: Travel by rail may be time consuming, but it is a fantastic way to see more of China. Foreigners usually travel 'soft class' and so can watch the scenery in comfort. 'Hard class' is less comfortable and more crowded.

The railway service in China is efficient and trains usually run on time and express services and sleepers are available.

Contact the Shanghai Railway Station on 242299.

By sea: Some cruise lines stop at Shanghai and the China Ocean Shipping Agency runs passenger ships between Shanghai and Hongkong and Shanghai and Kobe.

Help!

Consulates

Consular activities are listed below. These services exist by agreement with the host countries and are bound by certain local regulations, as well as by orders from their home countries.

Questions regarding:
- Visas and passports
- Difficulties with local regulations (Customs, the law, etc.)
- Assistance with absentee voting in home country
- Authorisation or witnessing of documents
- Assistance in case of death

Consulates are supposed to be notified in case of hospitalisation of a foreigner, if the nationality of the patient is known.

Your Consulate should be notified if you are involved in any type of accident whilst you are in China.

In case of arrest your Consulate should be notified.

Australia 70 Fuxing Rd.
France 1431 Huaihai Zhong Rd., tel: 377414
Japan 1517 Huaihai Zhong Rd., tel: 362073
Poland Anting Rd.
United States 1469 Huaihai Zhong Rd., tel: 379880
Germany Yong Fu Road, tel: 379953

Medical emergency telephones Shanghai

Hospital for Foreigners 530631

Police Emergencies

Shanghai is a fairly safe city and there is comparatively little crime. You should however watch out for pick-pockets and it is not a good idea to leave bags unattended. If you suspect that something has been stolen, report it immediately to your guide, hotel desk or to the police.

The police in China wear green uniforms with caps bearing the Chinese insignia. The uniform of the Chinese airforce is unfortunately very similar. In case of doubt the word for police is jingchá.

Death
The death of a foreign citizen requires immediate consultation with his/her embassy by friends, relatives, hospital or police authorities.

Lost Property
Items lost by foreigners are usually easily identifiable in China, so lost property should not be too much of a problem.

If you lose anything, or suspect that something has been stolen, report the loss/theft to the CITS office, to your guide or to hotel staff.

The loss or theft of passports or other important documents should be reported to your embassy.

Replacement of certain items

Airline tickets: report the loss/theft to the airline and request another ticket. Some proof of purchase may be needed before a replacement ticket will be issued.

Motoring

Car Hire

There are no self-drive rental cars available in Shanghai as the traffic, roads and road signs are just too much for the average tourist to cope with. You can however easily hire a chauffeur driven car. Ask at your hotel desk for particulars of car-hire companies or ask your CITS guide and they should be able to arrange something for you. If you only want a car for a few hours then you can always hire a taxi at an hourly rate.

Photography

Most types of camera film are available in the Friendship Store in Shanghai, but to be on the safe side you might like to pack a good supply of film. You can get your film processed in China, but most people prefer to wait until they get home to have their films developed.

One thing to remember in China is not to take pictures of individual people without first getting their permission.

> **INFOTIP:** Tourists are not permitted to take photographs of military personel or installations.

Post Offices

Most hotels have small post offices or a postal service desk where you can buy postcards, stamps and writing paper. These are usually open from 8am until 6pm from Mondays to Saturdays and from 8am until 12noon on Sundays.

Mail leaving China generally travels slowly. Surface mail takes a few months to arrive overseas and even airmail letters take about ten days.

Post restante. Chinese post offices do not have post restante facilities.

№: 0011

名称 尼龙花
Nylon Flower

№:

Publications

English: You can find a surprising number of English language publications available from newsstands in Shanghai's major hotels. There is the Asian Wall Street Journal, the International Herald Tribune, the China Daily, the China Pictorial and the Beijing Review; as well as Newsweek.

Books in English can often be bought in hotels as well as tourist books and translations of Chinese novels.

Maps: Free maps are available at hotels and tourist attractions and they are designed to help tourists find their way to various sightseeing spots.

Maps are also for sale at newsstands and bookshops which give more detailed street plans if you want to wander off the tourist trail.

Religious Services

Ask at your hotel desk for information about religious services. If you are in a tour group tell your guide of you intention of attending church so that you can make time for this in your schedule.

Restaurants and Nightlife

The Local Menu

Most hotels will serve breakfast from 7-9am, and you will often have a choice between Chinese or western food.

Lunch will usually be served between noon and 2pm and dinner is served early, usually from 6 to 8.30pm or 9 or 10pm for a banquet. Some hotels do keep their restaurants open later for foreigners who can't adjust but if you are planning a hectic day of sightseeing it might be better to get to bed early.

As for the food, China is famous for its cuisine and you will often find that Chinese food is very different from Chinese food back home.

One pleasant surprise is the sheer variety. If you are travelling from region to region you will have the opportunity to sample all sorts of local delights. Don't be put off by certain outlandish dishes, snake may feature on the menu but there is always much more to choose from.

When eating out it is best to do so in a group, that way you can try more dishes. Also remember that there are plenty of dishes to come so only take a small amount from each plate.

Shanghai has many wonderful restaurants so don't fall into the trap of only eating at your hotel. Go out and see for yourself why Shanghai is famed for its seafood of try one of Shanghai's many ethnic restaurants for a real treat. The following is a list of a few restaurants to get you started.

Shanghai

Lao Fandian 242 Fuzhou Road Shanghai
Lubolang 131 Yuyan Road Shanghai
Meilongzhen 22 Lane, 1081 Nanjing Road Shanghai
Shanghai Old Town Restaurant 242 Fuyou Road Shanghai
Szechuan Restaurant 457 Nanjing Road Shanghai
Chengdu Restaurant 795 Huaihai Zhong Shanghai
Luyangoun Restaurant 763 Nanjing Road Shanghai
Xinya 719 Nanjing Road Shanghai
Xinghualou 343 Fuzhou Road Shanghai
Youyi Jinjia 1000 Yan'an Zhong Road Shanghai
Yanyunlou 755 Nanjing Road Shanghai
Minjiang 679 Nanjing Road Shanghai
Zhiweiguan Restaurant 345 Fujian Zhong Shanghai
Meixan 314 Shaanxi Nan Road Shanghai
Renmin People's Restaurant 226 Nanjing Road Shanghai
Satay House 849 Huashan Road Shanghai
Moslem Restaurant 710 Fuzhou Road Shanghai
Kangle Restaurant 394 Huaihai Middle Road Shanghai
Red House Restaurant 37 Shanxi Road South Sanghai
Fast Food Service 74 Xixang Zhong Road Shanghai

Hangzhou

Dahua Restaurant 185 Nashan Road Hangzhou
Jiangcheng Restaurant Jiangcheng Lu Hangzhou
Qunying Renhe Road Hangzhou
Xintai Yan'an Road Hangzhou
Xinxin 78 Beishan Street Hangzhou
Xizi Zheda Road Hngzhou
Yan'an Restaurant Yan'an Road Hangzhou
Zhanghua Restaurant Youdian Road Hangzhou

> **INFOTIP:** Nearly all hotels offer Chinese and Western Cuisine. Most major hotels have disco or jazz music. (See also Part II, Hitting the High Spots)

Shopping

You should have many opportunities to shop in Shanghai, and even guided tours include shopping trips. Although tacky souvenirs can certainly be found in China you can also pick up some real bargains as prices in China tend to be much lower than they are in the west. The following descriptions may help you with your shopping.

Antiques: The export of antiques is strictly controlled in China. Only objects marked with a special wax seal can be taken out of the country, and these are all under 120 years old.

Bargains are also unlikely when buying antiques in Shanghai as dealers, and only a few are licensed to sell to foreigners, know exactly the value of the goods found in their shops.

However, you can look even if you can't buy and antique shops make wonderful sightseeing.

Bamboo Products: You will find all sorts of things made from bamboo in Shanghai, from delicate chopsticks and fans to furniture.

Bronzeware: Bronze vases, bowls and plates can be bought cheaply in Shanghai, and many of these are engraved in extravagant designs.

Carpets and Rugs: Wool or silk oriental rugs are popular tourist buys. Shop around a little before you buy to get the best price, and if possible buy from a large store which can arrange shipping.

Chops: Chops or seals are used by the Chinese instead of written signatures. They are made from ivory, jade, wood, stone or plastic and have the characters which form a name carved on their base. By pressing the base into ink and then onto a sheet of paper you produce an instant signature. You can have your own name carved onto a chop in Chinese characters for a unique souvenir.

Chopsticks: You can buy all kinds of chopsticks in Shanghai. Choose from a range of plain chopsticks or try the gorgeously painted chopsticks which come in their own little boxes. Chopsticks are practical souvenirs if you plan to be cooking and eating Chinese food when you get back home. The longer, thicker chopsticks are used for cooking.

Cloissoné: Chinese cloisonné is of a very high standard and is used on a variety of objects. Enamelware jewellery, plates and vases are all good buys.

Fabrics: China's silks and cottons are of exceptional quality and are also inexpensive. You can choose from a wide variety of colours and prints and buy the fabric by the metre or already made up into blouses, scarfs and dresses.

Fans: Millions of fans are produced in China each year. Many are mass-produced and 'cheap and nasty' but you will also find beautifully made wooden and paper fans.

Figurines: Colourful, quaint figurines of animals or historic or legendary figures are popular in China and can be bought from shops or souvenir stalls.

Furniture: When buying furniture in Shanghai look out for quality in the materials used and in the work. Carved wooden furniture is an especially evocative reminder of China. When buying furniture it is best to buy from a store which can arrange shipping.

Ginseng: Ginseng is famous in China for its medicinal properties, and you might like to try it for yourself. The best ginseng tends to be expensive, but remember that it can be bought more cheaply in Shanghai than in the herbalist stores in Hongkong.

Herbs and Spices: Look for spice stalls in the markets, they stock a bewildering array of exotic herbs and seasonings; some of which can only be found in certain regions of China. If you want to take any of these spices home check your country's import regulations first as many nations restrict the importation of plant products.

Kites: Shanghai can be quite windy so you will find a variety of kites available there. The kites can be very simple or very elaborate in their design and they make wonderful take home gifts for children.

Lacquerware: Lacquerware plates, cups, trays and boxes make attractive and practical souvenirs – especially if you enjoy Chinese food. If you develop a taste for Chinese tea look out for beautiful lacquerware tea services.

Luggage: Inexpensive suitcases and bags are good buys in Shanghai if you are facing the problem of having bought more than will fit in your own bags in China.

Musical Instruments: You can buy both Chinese and Western instruments in Shanghai at very good prices.

Paintings: Both original paintings and hand-drawn copies of ancient paintings can be bought in Shanghai. These come in scrolls and are very good as souvenirs and gifts.

Papercuts: Papercuts are delicate pieces of artwork made with scissors. They make decorative souvenirs.

Porcelain: Porcelain in China is described as being first, second or third class. The Chinese numerals for one, two and three are printed on the price tag so you can be sure of the quality of porcelain you are buying.

Reproductions: In Shanghai there are available many reproductions of museum pieces and archeological treasures. These can be bought from shops, souvenir stalls or museums.

Rubbings: Stone rubbings taken from temples or ancient carvings are popular souvenirs.

Souvenirs: Chinese dolls, clothing and posters – in short a whole range of souvenir items – can be found in stores and markets all over Shanghai.

Tea: If you develop a fondness for Chinese teas you can buy a whole range to take home and enjoy. Make sure though that the teas are packaged in accordance with the customs regulations of your own country.

Toys: China produces many kinds of children's toys which are both inexpensive and durable.

Woollens: Chinese woollens are inexpensive and a good range of cashmere sweaters are also available in Shanghai. The style of woollen clothing which can be found in Shanghai is also improving so while you cannot expect anything too new and exciting you can pick up quality woollen scarves and jumpers at good prices.

Where To Shop

Friendship Stores: Friendship Stores came about as places where export goods could be sold to foreigners but they now also stock imported goods for the benefit of foreign residents of Shanghai. Now for tourists convenience they also carry Chinese goods which are not intended for export – the type of thing you would find in any Chinese shop.

The advantages of shopping in a Friendship Store are that the staff will usually speak a little English and that you should be able to use your credit card there. Friendship stores are also less crowded than the local stores and their wares are usually of good quality. A major advantage is that staff will arrange to have any large purchases crated and shipped home for you, and you can also change foreign currency at Friendship Stores.

Friendship Store disadvantages are the prices, while they may seem reasonable the same goods may be available elsewhere for much less. You also miss out on seeing how the locals shop in a Friendship Store.

The Shanghai Friendship Store is located at 33 Zhongshan Dong-1 Road; tel: 210183.

Souvenir Shops: Souvenir shops are scattered all over Shanghai and sell a variety of souvenirs, some of which are mass-produced and awful and other which are of reasonable quality.

The best of the souvenir shops are found in handicraft factories and usually sell attractive and well-made goods.

Department Stores: You can buy a wide range of goods in Shanghai's department stores, though don't expect quite the same range of luxury items as you would find in the west.

You may find that to buy some items, such as fabrics, in department stores you will need ration coupons. Your guide may be able to get these for you but this would be very difficult, so try the Friendship Store first.

At 830 Nanjing Dong Road you will find the Number One Department Store which is visited by thousands of people each day. It is considered to be the biggest and best department store in Shanghai.

Free Markets: You can buy almost anything at a free market, including handicrafts, clothing, jewellery and furniture.

The Shi Luo Pu markets are Shanghai's largest so do your bargain hunting there.

Nanjing Road: Nanjing Road is Shanghai's main shopping street and you will find some wonderful speciality shops in the Nanjing Road area.

The Shanghai Arts and Crafts Store (tel:216529) is located at 190 Nanjing Xi road and the Friendship Store antique branch is located at number 694.

Along Nanjing Dong Road you will find the Shanghai Silk Shop (number 592) and the Shanghai Jewellery and Jade Store (number 438).

Shopping Hours

In Shanghai Friendship Stores and department stores open from 9am until 7 or 8pm, seven days a week. Smaller, local shops occasionally stay open until later.

Free Market

Sports and Athletics

Government policy is to encourage sport and the Chinese people, especially the young, are quick to take advantage of any sporting facility available. They show an immense dedication and can be fiercely competitive.

Athletics and Gymnastics
Are basic school and university activities and the more proficient go onto major competitions.

Basketball
Very popular sport and in international matches China can field teams of surprising height.

Table Tennis or Ping Pong
This is the speciality of the Chinese. This social game has been turned in China into one of skill, tactics and adroid athleticism.

Tai Ji Quan or Tai Chi
Tai Chi is attributed with keeping the body supple. Anywhere in China, first thing in the morning you will see young and old going through the intricate and slow routine.

Xiang Qi
Similar to Western game of Chess, dating from the eighteenth century AD, is one game you see played often.

Tiao Qi
Is played with marbles and a board with holes, we know it as the Chinese Checkers.

Mah Jong
This is a simple form of draughts very popular to pass the time.

Telephone and Telegraph

Local calls

Local calls can be made from public telephone booths or from your hotel room. The cost of making a local call from a coin-operated telephone is only a few fen.

Long Distance and Overseas Calls

Long distance or international calls have to be placed through an operator. These calls can be booked at your hotel and you can take the call at the hotel service desk or in your room. Hotels can arrange reverse charge calls.

Service Numbers:
Information 114
Long-distance information 116
Overseas operator 337431
Domestic long-distance operator 330100   331230

USEFUL PHRASE: Where is the telephone?
Diàn-hug zài nǎr?

Time

GMT plus 8 hours

Tipping

Tipping has now reached China. It is now customary to tip as you would in the West. As well as the national guide who accompanies you throughout China, your local guide should also be looked after as the world can easily be spread along the grapevine and the service you get in later cities may not be what you would expect.

Travel Services

China Golden Bridge, Travel Service, Shanghai Branch
2400 Siping Street
Tel 485344   Telex 33913 BIHLT CN

China Youth, Travel Service, Shanghai Branch
2 Hengsham Road
Tel 599791   Telex 33532 SYTS

Shanghai Oriental, Travel Service
371 Nanjing Road (West)
Tel 582057 or 587389

Shanghai Spring and Autumn International, Travel Service
342 Xizang Road (M)
Tel 221191 or 220097 or 207232
Telex 33909BTHHF CN

China Travel & Tourism Service Co., Shanghai Branch
S. Suzhou Road
Tel 219882

Aiqiao Travel Service
Sichuan N Road
Tel 251746

Asia (Yazhou) Travel Service
Nanjing W Road
Tel 537750

China International Travel Service, Shanghai Branch
33 Zhongshan Dongyi Road
Tel 217200
Telex 33277 SCITS CN or 33022 TRMCO CN
Fax 213370

China Travel Service, Shanghai Branch
Yan'an M Road
Tel 378521

Fengguang Travel Service
Ruijin Road
Tel 376572

Jiangshan Co-Op Travel Service
W Baoxing Road
Tel 628092

Shanghai Overseas Chinese Travel Service
Yan'an M Road
Tel 378521

Shanghai Travel Service
Fuzhou Road
Tel 221469 or 220904

Shanghai Youth Travel Service
Xiziang S Road
Tel 284566

Toilets

Toilets tend to be rather primitive in China, and worse is the lack of cubicle doors (or even cubicles). Always carry tissues and soap, as many public toilets do not have paper or soap.

Tourist Services

The China International Travel Service or Luxingshe looks after all tourists in China to some extent and it is through the CITS that tours are organised and accommodation arranged.

If you have any problems in China and would like to contact the CITS just ask your guide or your hotel desk for the nearest office.

Beijing: 6 Chang'an Dong Ave., tel: 551031
Shanghai: 33 Zhongshan Road E; tel: 324960
Overseas:
China Tourist Office, 4 Glentworth St., London NW1, ENGLAND
Office Du Tourisme de Chine, 51 Rue Sainte-anne 75002, FRANCE
China Tourist Office, Eschenheimer Anlage 28, D-6000 Frankfurt am Main-1, FEDERAL REPUBLIC OF GERMANY
China Tourist Office, 6F, Hachidai Hamamatsucho Bl. 1-27-13, Hamatsu-cho, Minato-ku, Tokyo, JAPAN
China Tourist Office, Lincoln Building, 60 E. 42nd St., Suite 465, New York, N.Y. 10165, U.S.A.

PART V
Business Guide

BUSINESS GUIDE

Business Briefing

Main Industries: textiles, toys, clothing, small appliances
Main agricultural products: rice, poultry, pork
Main imports: cereals, rolled steel, fertilisers, machinery, sugar, unprocessed cotton
Main exports: crude oil, refined petroleum products, textiles, clothing, canned goods, coal, fruit and vegetables
Principle trading parters: Hongkong Japan, USA, West Germany, Jordan, Canada

Exchange/Import and Export of Currency

Chinese currency could not be taken in or out of China.

However, there is no limit to the amount of Foreign currency which may be brought into China.

That will be exchanged for Foreign Exchange Certificates which can be changed back to Foreign currency on departure.

Banks

Foreign Banks in Shanghai
BANK OF TOKYO, tel: 582582X58135
BANQUE NATIONALE DE PARIS, tel: 582582X58142

Chinese Banks

BANK OF CHINA, tel: 217466
CHARTERED BANK, tel: 218858
HONGKONG SHANGHAI BANKING CORPORATION, tel: 218383

Banking Hours

Most hotels have foreign exchange offices which are open from 7.30 or 8am until 7pm, though the hours depend upon the size of the hotel. Larger hotels designed with western tourists in mind have foreign exchange offices which stay open later.

Credit Cards

Nearly all major credit cards are accepted by hotels in China

Translators and Interpreters

All major hotels offer translator and interpreter services they are all equipped with telex and nearly all with fax facilities.

Conference and Secreterial Services

Most hotels have various conference rooms and a multi-function hall. Business centres are readily available to cater for the needs of international businessmen.

> **INFOTIP:** Don't hesitate to ask the hotel reception for any business needs that you might have you will be pleasantly surprised.

Alphabetical Index

Index

Notes

Notes